GERMAN-ENGLISH
ENGLISH-GERMAN

Dictionary and Phrasebook

GERMAN-ENGLISH
ENGLISH-GERMAN

Dictionary and Phrasebook

MICHAEL JELDEN

HIPPOCRENE BOOKS
New York

ISBN 0-7818-0857-X

For information, contact:

Hippocrene Books, Inc.
171 Madison Avenue
New York, NY 10016

Cataloging-in-Publication Data available from the Library of Congress.

Printed in the United States of America.

CONTENTS

PREFACE

*T*his book has been written for those who might travel to a German-speaking country, or who want to prepare for a meeting with German-speaking people. It has been designed for use as a communication aid in most situations of everyday life.

In this book, a concise overview of German grammar and an introduction to German pronunciation is provided together with listings of the most frequently used words and many easy to combine phrases for everyday use. The two-way German-English/English-German dictionary includes over 5,000 total entries, while the phrasebook is composed of 23 chapters.

Since the pronunciation of German words is simple, once understood, I have not included the pronunciation of every word. Thus, the reader should carefully read the pronunciation guidelines.

The phrasebook section is divided into thematic blocks. Each of those blocks deals with one category of what travelers may need to communicate in various situations, in friendly as well as in unpleasant moments.

The reader will also find some general information about the German, Austrian, and Swiss people: their countries, customs, and local specialties.

It is my sincere hope that this book will not only be useful for those who want an introduction to the

German language, but also be entertaining reading for those who would like to have a little insight into German culture.

INTRODUCTION TO THE GERMAN LANGUAGE

The German language is very closely related to the English language, even if on first sight it may seem quite different. In the fifth century A.D., the Saxons started to conquer the British islands, which were then populated by the Celts. The conquerors brought with them their language, Saxon, that was very closely related to Old High German and that until then had been spoken in the area that is today the eastern part of Germany. Both languages then developed separately, into English (the modern Anglo-Saxon) and German. Influenced by their neighbors, each language formed its individual properties, such as changes in parts-of-speech and word building.

German is considered by many one of the more difficult languages of the world. Many stories circulate of people whose intent to learn the language only led to frustration. For somebody unfamiliar with it, the language can seem quite illogical, arbitrary, and extremely irregular. On becoming more acquainted with the language, however, one will discover that this is not the case. Certainly for an English speaker it is not as difficult to memorize German words, and to speak German, as is commonly believed. Both languages have similarities in their grammar structure and vocabulary. It is easy to see how closely related many English and German words are. Just look at examples like:

house	Haus*
man	Mann*
find	finden

drink	trinken
see	sehen

*N.B. All nouns are capitalized in German.

Carefully note the following examples:

sick	krank
sick**ness**	**Krank**heit
open	offen
open**ness**	Offen**heit**
observe	beobachten
observa**tion**	Beobach**tung**

In the left column it can be noted that when English nouns are formed from adjectives by adding -*ness*, the corresponding German substantive in the right column is formed by adding -*heit*, or where in English -*tion* is added to a verb, -*ung* is added in German. There are many such elementary rules that make it easy to trace German words and their forms and to build new words from already known ones. The most important of these rules will be explained in the grammar section of this book.

shi**p**	Schi**ff**
a**pp**le	A**pf**el
penny	**Pf**enning
boo**k**	Bu**ch**
si**t**	si**tz**en
to	**z**u

In the above columns you can observe that often when English has the sounds *p*, *k*, or *t*, German has *pf/f*, *ch*, or *tz/z*. The reason for this change is called the Old High German consonant shift, that occurred between the fourth and seventh centuries. It was only then that the predecessors of English and German clearly separated from each other. Before that time they did not show many more differences than are usually found between dialects, and their vocabulary is derived from the same roots.

German word order is relatively free, although subject-verb-object order is most frequently used.

One of the most significant differences between the English and German languages is found in the treatment of verbs. Most English infinitives are identical with the root, or stem, of the corresponding verb, while the German infinitive is formed by adding the ending *–en* to the verb root.

While in English only the 3rd person singular requires a change in the verb form, German verbs change in form for each subject, or all persons. These endings are consistent in the present and past tenses.

person	to play	spielen
1st singular	I play	ich spiel**e**
2nd singular	you play	du spiel**st**
3rd singular	he play**s**	er spiel**t**
1st plural	we play	wir spiel**en**
2nd plural	you (pl.) play	ihr spiel**t**
3rd plural	they play	sie spiel**en**

As in English, German verbs are divided in two categories: *weak* and *strong* verbs. In some tenses, strong verbs may have a change in the last vowel of their root, while weak verbs do not. An example is *I see - I saw*. In English this change can sometimes only be heard: note for example the difference in pronunciation of *ea* in both words, *I hear - I heard*. In German, however, this change is always written: *ich sehe - ich sah* (I see - I saw), or *ich gehe - ich ging* (I go - I went). As shown above, the root of a German verb is determined by deleting the infinitive ending *-en* (and any prefixes).

An English verb that is weak is often also weak in German, and English strong verbs are often also strong in German.

In all languages of the world some words are of greater significance than others because they are used more frequently. Words like *the, have, not, you, with, in* or *but* are essential in all languages, and it is hardly possible to form useful sentences without them. In German there are approximately 100 words that statistically make up over 50 percent of everyday language. These words will be given in a separate list, labeled "The 103 Most Used Words."

The German language has three genders: nouns and adjectives are either masculine, feminine, or neuter. Therefore German also has three articles: *der*, masculine, *die*, feminine, and *das*, neuter, all in place of the one English article *the*. Note that Old English, spoken around 1000 A.D. in England, also used three genders. These can still be traced in the 3rd person singular pronouns *he, she,* and *it*. The distinction between genders is not always logical, though in most cases it is easily possible to determine a word's gender with some helpful hints, for example *der Mann* (the man) is masculine, just as *die Frau* (the woman) is feminine. That is quite logically determined by nature. And yet *das Mädchen* (the girl) is neuter. One's first reaction in this case would be to assume an irregularity. But there is a simple reason for *Mädchen* being neuter: all substantives ending in *-chen* are diminutives, and diminutives are always neuter. *Das Mädchen* is the diminutive form of *die Maid*. The original German word, *Maid*, is antiquated and no longer in use, but note the similarity to English (the maid). Accordingly all words ending in *-heit* or *-keit* and all words ending in *-ung* and *-tion* (see above table) are feminine. The plural form of all articles is *die*.

I would like to encourage everyone to look not only at the translated phrases in this book, but also at the short grammar section. You will see that already a little knowledge of the most elementary basics of German grammar will enable you to derive hundreds of words and build sentences. It will also help you to communicate freely and with ease in many situations. German is not at all difficult for you, just go for it!

GERMAN ALPHABET AND PRONUNCIATION

*T*he German alphabet consists of 29 letters, including 21 consonants, 5 vowels, and 3 umlauts (modified vowels).

The pronunciation of German consonants is often quite similar to the corresponding English pronunciation. As in English, some sounds are represented by combinations of consonants, for example *tsch*, which indicates the *ch* sound in *couch*.

German vowels are generally pronounced like their English counterparts, except that they are never rounded. A German *o* will always be pronounced like *ou* in r*ou*gh or *o* in m*o*lest, whereas in the English word *go*, the *o* is pronounced like *ow* in sh*ow*. The umlauts are: *ä, ö, ü.*

German vowels can be combined to form diphthongs, combinations of a strong and a weak vowel. The most frequent are: *ai, au, ei, oi, ui.*

Double consonants generally affect the preceding vowel by shortening it. Double vowels generally lengthen the vowel: in the series *Sellerie* (celery) - *selten* (seldom) - *Seele* (soul), the emphasized *e* is gradually becoming longer. In *Sellerie* (celery) the *e* sound is nearly twice as short as in *selten* (seldom), while in *Seele* (soul) it is nearly twice as long.

There are, of course, regional differences and dialects that sometimes cause considerable differences in the pronunciation of German sounds. The standard pronunciation is given in the following table. Pronunciation is only explained when it differs from the standard English pronunciation of the letter.

Letter, Umlaut, or Diphthong	Pronunciation	Example(s)
a	like *a* in *f<u>a</u>ther*	Vater *father*
ai	like *i* in *s<u>i</u>de*	Mai *May*
au	like *ou* in *h<u>ou</u>se*	Haus *house*
ä	similar to *ea* in *d<u>ea</u>d*	Äpfel *apples*
b		Butter *butter*
c	*ts*, most frequently encountered in combinations	Cäsium *cesium* (a chemical element)
ch	like *ch* in Scottish *lo<u>ch</u>*	Loch *hole*
ck	like *k*, but the preceding vowel is shortened	hacken *to hack*
d		doppelt *double*
dsch	like *j* in *<u>j</u>ungle*	Dschungel *jungle*
e	like *e* in *g<u>e</u>t*, always unrounded	elegant *elegant*
ei	like *i* in *s<u>i</u>de*	Seite *side*
f		fein *fine*
g	like *gh* in *<u>gh</u>ost*	Gast *guest*
h		Hotel *hotel*
i	like *i* in *b<u>i</u>t*	wissen *to know*
j	like *y* in *<u>y</u>ear*	Jahr *year*
k	like *c* in *<u>c</u>onvent*	kommen *come*
l	German *l* is pronounced with relaxed tongue, like an English initial clear *l*. It is never rounded like *ll* in *he<u>ll</u>o*.	leicht *light*

m		Mann *man*
n		Nase *nose*
o	like *o* in *molest*	offen *open*
ö	The *ö*-sound can be produced by saying *e* through closely rounded lips, similar to French *feu*.	Öffnung *opening*
p		Papier *paper*
ph	like *ph* in *philosophy*	phantastisch *fantastic*
q	[Like in English] *q* in German appears only in combination with *u*. It is pronounced with more of a *v* – sound, like *kv*.	Quecksilber *quicksilver*
r	*r* can be pronounced in three ways:	
	(1) With the tip of the tongue, as in Italian or Spanish.	(1) Ratte *rat*
	(2) The second way does not have an equivalent in English, but it sounds somewhat similar to *ch*, but softer, voiced. The root of the tongue is vibrating in the back part of the palate.	(2) arbeiten *work*
	(3) If *r* is not an initial (the first letter of a word) it can also be pronounced similar to *a*.	(3) erster *first*

s	like *s* in <u>S</u>aturday when:	<u>Voiceless:</u>
	(1) It is final (the last letter of a word).	(1) Gras *grass*
	(2) It is doubled.	(2) hassen *hate*
	(3) When it stands next to a voiceless consonant, such as *k*, *p*, *s*, *t*.	(3) bester *best*
	like English "z" when:	<u>Voiced:</u>
	(1) It is initial.	(1) Sonne *sun*
	(2) It is the first letter of a syllable.	(2) Rose *rose*
sch	like *sh* in <u>sh</u>oe	Schuh *shoe*
ß	like *ss*, the difference is merely an orthographic one. *ß* instead of *ss* stands after a shortened vowel, if it is not followed by another vowel.	Haß *hatred*
t		tanzen *dance*
tsch	like *ch* in <u>ch</u>ance	tschechisch *Czech*
tz	like *ts* in hi<u>ts</u> This is the same sound as *z*. This sound is always written *tz* when it is not the initial sound in the word.	Hitze *heat*
u	like *oo* in b<u>oo</u>t	unter *under*
ü	This sound can be produced by saying *i* through closely rounded lips, similar to French s<u>u</u>r.	über *over*

v	like *f*	voll *full*
w	voiced equivalent to *f*, similar to <u>v</u>ast or <u>v</u>ague German *w* is never rounded like in English <u>water</u>.	Wasser *water*
x		Xylophon *xylophone*
y	like *y* in <u>y</u>acht or German *j*	Yacht *yacht*
z	like *z* in <u>z</u>one	Zimt *cinnamon*

Orthography

In addition to the first word of each sentence, nouns, verbal nouns, and proper names are capitalized. It is usually very easy to understand how a written word is pronounced, and vice versa; thus, you will not find it too hard to write a word that you have heard spoken.

ABBREVIATIONS

A	Österreich (Austria)
acc.	accusative
art.	article
CH	Schweiz (Switzerland)
conj.	conjunction
D	Deutschland (Germany)
dat.	dative
f	feminine
m	masculine
n	neuter
pl.	plural
pr.	pronoun
refl. pr.	reflective pronoun
rel. pr.	relative pronoun
s.	singular
V	weak verb
V*	strong verb
V1	verb, that (1) requires the past participle prefix *ge* between the verbal prefix (a preposition) and the stem and that (2) separates the verbal prefix from the stem in present and past tense active.
$V^*1 = V^* + V1$	
V2	verbs that do not form their past participle with the prefix *ge*.
→	see

A BASIC GRAMMAR

*I*n the following section the most important rules and their exceptions will be shown. Some points of German grammar can be fairly complicated. These, however, do not have to be mastered in order to form and understand simple sentences and questions.

➤ Articles

All German nouns are accompanied by a definite or indefinite article. The article must agree in number and gender with the noun or pronoun to which it refers. [As mentioned before, German has three genders: masculine, feminine, and neuter.] Note that definite and indefinite articles have the same plural forms in all genders. In addition, articles are declined according to the case of the corresponding noun or pronoun.

Definite articles:

the	*masculine singular*	*feminine singular*	*neuter singular*	*all genders plural*
nominative	der	die	das	die
accusative	de**n**	die	das	die
dative	de**m**	de**r**	de**m**	de**n**
genitive	des	de**r**	des	de**r**

Many pronouns are declined the same way as German indefinite articles. In order to show this,

the declined endings of each article are emphasized
in bold.

Indefinite articles:

a, an	masculine singular	feminine singular	neuter singular	all genders plural
nominative	ein	eine	ein(es[1])	einige
accusative	ein	eine	ein	einige
dative	einem	einer	einem	einigen
genitive	eines	einer	eines	einiger

1. *eines* is used if the pronoun stands alone.

➤ Pronouns

Due to the limited space for grammar topics in this
little book, only the most important pronouns are
shown here: personal pronouns (*I, you . . .*), possessive
pronouns (*my, your, his . . .*), interrogative pronouns
(*who, what . . .*), indefinite pronouns (*someone, something . . .*), reflexive pronouns (*myself, yourself . . .*) and
relative pronouns (*that, who . . .*).

Personal pronouns:

Polite form: When addressing someone with whom
one is not particularly familiar, a formal, polite pronoun, *Sie*, is always used instead of the informal *du*
(you). *Sie* is both the singular and plural polite form
for "you" and when used, the verb is conjugated in

the 3rd person singular (or plural, if more than one person is addressed). Note that this pronoun is always capitalized when written.

	1st s. I	2nd s. you	3rd s. he/she/it
nominative	ich	du	er/sie/es; Sie
accusative	-[1]	-	-
dative	mir	dir	ihm/ihr/ihm; Ihnen
genitive	-[2]	-	-

	1st pl. we	2nd pl. you	3rd pl. they
nominative	wir	ihr	sie[1]; Sie
accusative	-	-	-
dative	uns	euch	ihnen; ihm; Ihnen
genitive	-	-	-

1. The accusative of personal pronouns are the reflexive pronouns.
2. The genitive of personal pronouns are the possessive pronouns.

Possessive pronouns:

Possessive, reflexive, and indefinite pronouns are declined like indefinite articles. For example, *ein* is the masculine nominative indefinite article and *mein* is the masculine nominative possessive pronoun. The possessive pronoun always agrees in gender with that which is possessed (not the possessor).

In the following table only the masculine forms are shown. Feminine and neuter forms of possessive pronouns are built analogous to the corresponding forms of indefinite articles. For example, *ein* and *mein* in the example above are masculine, and in the table of indefinite articles, you can see that the masculine *ein* becomes the feminine *eine*; in the same way, *mein* becomes *meine*. Note that the neuter 3rd person singular form is always identical to the 3rd person masculine form and thus not shown in the table.

The following forms are for possessed objects in the singular:

	1st s. *my*	*2nd s.* *your*	*3rd s.* *his/her; your* *(polite)*
nominative	mein	dein	sein/ihr; Ihr
accusative	meinen	deinen	seinen, ihren; Ihren
dative	meinem	deinem	seinem/ ihrem; Ihrem
genitive	meines	deines	seines/ihres; Ihres

	1st pl. *our*	*2nd pl.* *your*	*3rd pl.* *their; your* *(pl. polite)*
nominative	unser	euer	ihr[1]; Ihr
accusative	unseren	euren	ihren; Ihren
dative	unserem	eurem	ihrem; Ihrem
genitive	unseres	eures	ihres; Ihres

1. Like the indefinite articles, possessive pronouns have only one plural form for all three genders.

The following forms are for possessed objects in the plural:

	my	your	his/her; you (polite)
nominative	meine	deine	seine/ihre; Ihre
accusative	meine	deine	seine, ihre; Ihre
dative	meinen	deinen	seinen, ihren; Ihren
genitive	meiner	deiner	seiner/ihrer; Ihrer

	our	your (pl.)	their; your (pl. polite)
nominative	unsere	eure	ihre; Ihre
accusative	unsere	eure	ihre; Ihre
dative	unseren	euren	ihren; Ihren
genitive	unserer	eurer	ihrer; Ihrer

Interrogative pronouns:

Interrogative pronouns are used to form qualifying questions that cannot be answered with *yes* or *no*. The most frequently used interrogative pronouns are:

who	*wer*
what	*was*
whose	*wessen*
to whom (*dat.*), whom	*wem*
whom (*acc.*)	*wen*
where	*wo*
how	*wie*
where to	*wohin*
from where	*woher*

when	*wann*
how many	*wie viele*
how much	*wieviel*

Indefinite pronouns:

Indefinite pronouns are used when you do not want to or cannot determine exactly the subject of the sentence. Some indefinite pronouns can be used instead of nouns and can serve as the subject of a sentence. In a German sentence they function exactly as in an English sentence. The most frequently used indefinite pronouns are:

somebody/someone	*jemand*
anybody	*irgendwer, irgend jemand*
somehow	*irgendwie*
somewhere	*irgendwo*
something	*etwas*
anything	*irgend etwas, irgendwas*
some	*etwas, einige*
every	*alle, alles*
everybody	*jeder*
everywhere	*überall*
one, you, people[1]	*man*
nobody	*niemand*
nowhere	*nirgendwo*
never	*nie, niemals*

1. *man* is usually translated as *one, you* or *people*. It is used whenever you talk about people in general, e.g. ***Man** kann den Berggipfel sehen! **You** can see the top of the mountain!*, or ***One** can see the top of the mountain!*

Reflexive pronouns:

Reflexive pronouns do not change according to gender.

	myself	*yourself*	*him-/her-/itself; yourself* (polite)
Reflexive pronouns	mich	dich	sich[1]; sich[2]

	ourselves	*yourselves*	*themselves; yourselves* (pl. polite)
Reflexive pronouns	uns	euch	sich[1]; sich[2]

1. For all genders.
2. Not capitalized.

Relative pronouns:

The relative pronouns that refer to persons, animals, or things, such as *that* and *who,* take the gender of the subject to which they refer. They are *der, die,* and *das* for masculine, feminine, and neuter genders respectively; therefore, *The man,* **who** . . . *Der Mann,* **der** . . . , or *The horse,* **that** . . . *Das Pferd,* **das** . . . , since *Der Mann* is masculine and *Das Pferd* is neuter.

➤ Nouns

Plural:

The endings *-er, -n, -e* or *-s* are added to form the plural of a noun, e.g. *die Katze* (the cat), plural *die*

Katzen. In some words the last vowel of the stem changes into an umlaut, e.g. *das Haus* (the house), plural *die Häuser* (the houses).

Nouns ending in *-el* and *-er* build their plural forms by adding *-n* to the stem, if they are feminine. Masculine and neuter nouns ending in *-el* and *-er* are identical in singular and plural, e.g. *das Fenster* (the window), plural *die Fenster*; *der Stecker* (the plug), plural *die Stecker*. Note that a stem vowel change can occur also in this case, e.g. *der Hammer* (the hammer), plural *die Hämmer*.

Declination of nouns:

Of the four existing cases in modern German only the genitive case has to be marked on the noun, just as in English. Its ending for masculine and neuter nouns is *-es* or *-s*. Feminine words remain unchanged in the genitive case.

Words that end in *-s*, *-ß*, *-z*, *-tz* or *-x* and words that consist of only one syllable have the genitive ending *-es*. In most other cases, especially when the word ends in a vowel, the ending is *-s*, but frequently both forms can be used. The difference, grammatically and in pronunciation, is so slight that you can just use the one that fits better in your opinion.

Examples:
Das Haus (the house), genitive: *des Hauses*
Der Mann (the man), genitive: *des Mannes*
Die Frau (the woman), genitive: *der Frau*

Some declination patterns (see above for the corresponding articles):

	masculine singular	the man plural
nominative	Mann	Männer[1]
accusative	Mann	Männer
dative	Mann; Manne[2]	Männern
genitive	Mannes	Männer

	feminine singular	the cat plural
nominative	Katze	Katzen
accusative	Katze	Katzen
dative	Katze	Katzen
genitive	Katze	Katzen

	neuter singular	the child plural
nominative	Kind	Kinder
accusative	Kind	Kinder
dative	Kind	Kindern
genitive	Kindes	Kinder

1. Transformation of the stem's last vowel *a* to the umlaut *ä*, as mentioned above.
2. The dative form *dem Manne* is a somewhat old-fashioned form, but in some regions it is still in use.

➤ Adjectives and Adverbs

Adjectives are declined in the same way as nouns.

Adverbs are not marked on the German word, i.e. their form is identical to the corresponding adjective.

Comparison of adjectives:

The first grade of comparison—the comparative—is formed just like the English comparative, i.e. by adding *er* to the adjective: *neu - neuer,* (new - new**er**). The superlative is built by adding *-sten* or *-esten* and is always preceded by the particle *am*: newest - *am neuesten*. Note that *gut* (good) has the irregular comparative *besser* (better).

➤ Verbs

The main challenges in learning German are encountered in verbal conjugation. A number of German verbs, and especially the most frequently used ones, are irregular.

Every German infinitive ends in *-en*. This ending is added to the root of the verb. German verbs occur in the indicative, subjunctive and conditional modes in one present tense, three past tenses, and two future tenses, for the active and passive voice. German does not have an equivalent to English continuous forms such as *I am going* or *I was eating*. Simple forms are used instead. The most common past tense form is the perfect past tense, which is composed of an auxiliary verb + past participle. As in English, the second future (e.g. I *will have gone* to New York) is nearly extinct in everyday language.

Verbs can be divided into auxiliary verbs and proper verbs. Auxiliary verbs are used to build the perfect and pluperfect forms, and to describe other verbs more closely, e.g. *Ich **möchte** diesen Film sehen!* (I want to see this movie!), where *möchte* (want) is used as an auxiliary verb. Auxiliary verbs are conjugated just like proper verbs—except the exceptions, of course!

The most frequently used auxiliary verbs are *sein* (to be), *haben* (to have), *werden* (to become), *wollen/mögen* (to want), *können* (to be able to), *dürfen* (to be allowed to/may), *sollen* (to be supposed to/shall).

German verbs are either strong verbs or weak verbs (see Introduction). Strong verbs change the root vowel in past tense forms and in some present tense forms, but weak verbs remain unchanged. This is a property that many Germanic languages show, including English, such as in the past tense form of *see - saw*. Strong verbs are marked in the dictionary section (V^*).

One of the most characteristic features of German verbs is that preposition and verb merge into each other to form another verb, e.g. *kommen* **herein** (come **in**) becomes **hereinkommen.** Many of those verbs build their past participle by inserting the prefix *ge between* the merged preposition and the verb itself: *hereingekommen.* In the present and past tenses, however, these verbs split into two parts: (1) the preposition (*herein* in the above example) and (2) the verb base (*kommen* in the above example). In this case the verb base is conjugated as usual, and the preposition is treated just as a normal preposition, i.e. the verb is treated like in English: *Ich komme herein* (I come in); *Ich kam herein* (I came in). Note that this separation occurs only in the present and past tenses in active voice.

Those verbs are marked in the dictionary section (*V1*).

Conjugation patterns of proper verbs in active voice:

➤ *sagen* - to say (weak verb, stem: *sag*):

	pronoun	*present tense*	*past tense*
1ˢᵗ s.	ich	sage	sagte
2ⁿᵈ s.	du	sagst	sagtest
3ʳᵈ s.	er/sie/es	sagt	sagte
1ˢᵗ pl.	wir	sagen	sagten
2ⁿᵈ pl.	ihr	sagt	sagtet
3ʳᵈ pl.	sie; Sie	sagen	sagten

➤ *reden* - to talk (weak verb, stem: *red*):

	pronoun	*present tense*	*past tense*
1ˢᵗ s.	ich	rede	redete
2ⁿᵈ s.	du	redest	redetest
3ʳᵈ s.	er/sie/es	redet	redete
1ˢᵗ pl.	wir	reden	redeten
2ⁿᵈ pl.	ihr	redet	redetet
3ʳᵈ pl.	sie; Sie	reden	redeten

➤ *sehen* - to see (strong verb, stem: *seh*, strong stem: *sah*):

	pronoun	*present tense*	*past tense*
1ˢᵗ s.	ich	sehe	sah
2ⁿᵈ s.	du	siehst	sahst
3ʳᵈ s.	er/sie/es	sieht	sah
1ˢᵗ pl.	wir	sehen	sahen
2ⁿᵈ pl.	ihr	seht	saht
3ʳᵈ pl.	sie; Sie	sehen	sahen

Many verbs, especially those with stems that end in a consonant, insert a vowel between their root and the ending, in the above example *reden* an *-e* (red**e**st).

From the above tables you see that the sign of the past tense of weak verbs is *et/t* between the stem and the ending, and that each person has its specific endings.

For perfect and past tense forms the past participle is required. The past participle of strong verbs is built by adding *ge-* to the infinitive: *sehen* (to see), past participle: *gesehen*. Weak verbs add the same prefix to the 3rd person singular present tense active form: *reden* (to talk), past participle: *geredet.*

In some cases the past participle is identical to the infinitive. Those cases are marked in the dictionary section (*V2*).

Some other verbs have irregular past participles, like *gehen* (to go), past participle *gegangen*, or *haben* (to have), past participle *gehabt.*

The perfect, pluperfect and future tenses are built with present, past and future forms of the auxiliary verbs *sein* (to be) and *haben* (to have), combined with the past participle (for perfect and pluperfect tenses) or the infinitive (for the future tense):

	pronoun	***perfect tense***	***pluperfect tense***	***future tense***
1st s.	ich	habe geredet	hatte geredet	werde reden
2nd s.	du	hast geredet	hattest geredet	wirst reden
3rd s.	er/sie/es	hat geredet	hatte geredet	wird reden

	pronoun	perfect tense	pluperfect tense	future tense
1ˢᵗ pl.	wir	haben geredet	hatten geredet	werden reden
2ⁿᵈ pl.	ihr	habt geredet	hattet geredet	werdet reden
3ʳᵈ pl.	sie; Sie	haben geredet	hatten geredet	werden reden

➤ Conditional

The present and past conditionals are also formed with an auxiliary verb. The present conditional is formed with the conditional form of *sein* (to be) and an infinitive; the past conditional is formed with the conditional form of *haben* (to have) and the past participle.

The conditional of *reden* (to speak):

	pronoun	present conditional	past conditional
1ˢᵗ s.	ich	würde reden	hätte geredet
2ⁿᵈ s.	du	würdest reden	hättest geredet
3ʳᵈ s.	er/sie/es	würde reden	hätte geredet
1ˢᵗ s.	wir	würden reden	hätten geredet
2ⁿᵈ pl.	ihr	würdet reden	hättet geredet
3ʳᵈ pl.	sie; Sie	würden reden	hätten geredet

➤ Passive Voice

Passive forms are built with the auxiliary verb *werden* (to become) and the past participle.

Of course, German verbs are much more complicated than this overview. But knowing these elementary elements of grammar you will be able to express yourself very well, because you will have the ability to relate every possible concept in the German language. The most important verb forms are present tense, perfect tense, and present conditional. If you don't want to learn too much grammar . . . these three tenses will do it for you.

➤ Syntax

German word order is in general the same as in English. The first element of a statement is the subject of the sentence, followed by a genitive attribute if present, the predicate, one or more objects and further parts of the sentence (SPO). In subordinated clauses the word order is SOP.

*Der Garten des Schlosses **ist** sehr schön.*
The garden of the castle **is** very beautiful.

*Ich **kannte** das Mädchen, das wir gestern **getroffen haben**.*
I **knew** the girl, whom we **met** last night.

*Ich **gebe** meinem Sohn einen Apfel und die Zeitschrift, die ich gestern **gekauft habe**.*
I **give** my son an apple and the magazine I **bought** this morning.

Please note that the verb is sometimes split (see Verbs).

Adverbs usually stand close to the corresponding verb, and some adverbs (especially adverbs of time) can also start a sentence.

***Gestern** waren wir in Berlin.*
Yesterday we were in Berlin.

*Du hast die Frage **schnell** beantwortet.*
You have answered the question **quickly**.

Interrogative sentences usually start with the predicate, followed by one or more objects and the subject.

Hast** du sie den Baum hinunterfallen **sehen?
Did you **see** her falling down the tree?

If interrogative sentences start with an interrogative pronoun such as *who, where,* or *what,* the pronoun begins the sentence.

***Wer** gab dem kind einen Apfel?*
Who gave the child an apple?

The imperative also follows the verb - subject - object order.

Geben Sie dem kind einen Apfel bitte!
Give the child an apple please!

Negative clauses are formed by using the negative article *kein* (none) or by inserting *nicht* (not).

English participle constructions must be converted into infinitive constructions or subordinated clauses. The position of the beginning of subordinated clauses (like relative clauses) is determined by the part of the main sentence to which the subordinated clause refers. This might sound complicated, but it is just the same as in English.

Obwohl er sie in einer Konferenz <u>kennengelernt hatte</u>,
    *konnte Franz sich an ihren Namen **nicht erinnern**.*
Though <u>having met her</u> once in a meeting, Franz
    could not remember her name.

You will find examples of most types of sentences in the phrasebook section.

➤ Making New Words

It is easy to make new words from known ones. Word building often follows the same rules in German than in English. For example, this means that when forming English nouns from adjectives by adding the ending *–ness*, you usually would add *–heit* or *–keit* to the end of a corresponding German adjective.

Making nouns from adjectives:

English	German
-ness	-heit; -keit

Examples: lazy**ness** - Faul**heit**

Making nouns from verbs:

Use the German infinitive with the neuter article *das*.

Making adjectives from nouns:

English	German
-ish, -ly	-lich
-less	-los

Examples: yellow**ish** – gelb**lich**
          sense**less** – sinn**los**.

Diminutives:

If you want to express that something is small, or smaller than usual, or that something is especially cute you can use the diminutive endings *–chen* or *–lein*.

Examples: chair - Stuhl, little chair – Stühl**chen**;
book – Buch, little book – Büch**lein**.

Note that here, also, sometimes the last vowel of the
stem is transformed into an umlaut.

THE TOP 103 WORDS

*T*he following 103 words compose up to fifty percent of any everyday German conversation. The most frequently encountered of these words are the articles *der / die / das* (the), *ein* (a), and the verb *sein* (to be).

Some of these words occur most frequently in idiomatic structures. These words are marked by a number and explained below the table.

The following list is sorted alphabetically:

aber	but
alle	every, all
als	when; as
an / am	at / at the (1)
andere	other
auch	too, also
auf	on
aus	from, out of
bei	at, near
beide	both
besser	better
bis	until, 'til
*bleiben V**	to stay, remain
bringen	to bring
da	there; because, since (2)
damit	so that, in order to; with it
dann	then
daß	*conj.* that (3)
der / die / das	*art.* the; *rel. pr.* who, that
dieser	this, that
durch	by; through

dürfen V	to be allowed to, may
ein	a; one
er / sie / es	*pr.* he / she / it
erst / zuerst	at first
etwas	something
Frage f die	question
fragen V	to ask
für	for
geben V*	to give
gegen	against
gehen V*	to go
groß	big, large
gut	good, well
haben V	to have
Haus n das	house
heute	today
hier	here
hoch	high
ich	*pr.* I
ihr	*pr.* you
immer	always
in / im	in (1)
jede	every
jetzt	now
kein	no, none
klein	small
kommen V*	to come
können V*	to be able to, can, may
lassen V*	to let, allow
letzte	last
Leute pl. die	people *pl.* (4)
machen V	to make, do
man	people; one
mehr	more
mein	my
mit	with

müssen $V^\star$	must, to have to
nach	after, later
nehmen $V^\star$	to take
neu	new
nicht	not
noch	still, yet (5)
nur	only
oder	or
ohne	without
sagen V	to say
schnell	fast, quickly
schon	already
schön	beautiful, nice
sehen $V^\star$	to see
sehr	very
sein $V^\star$	to be
sein / ihr	*pr.* his / her
seit	since
so	so
sollen V	shall, be to
sondern	but
sprechen $V^\star$	to speak
stehen $V^\star$	to stand
Tag m der	day
tun V	to do, make
über	over; about
um	around; about
und	and
unter	under
viel	many
von / vom	from; by; of / from the; by the; of the (1)
vor	before
was	what; that (6)
weil	because
weiter	farther

wenig	few
wenn	if, whether
wer	who
werden V★	to become
wie	how
wieder	again
wir	we
wissen V★	to know
wollen V	to want
Zeit f die	time
zu / zum	to / to the (1)
zwei	two
zwischen	between

(1) The word after the slash (/) is the combination of the conjunction and the masculine article, e.g. *an dem = am*.
(2) *da* is sometimes used instead of *weil* (because).
(3) *that* as a conjunction, for example: I didn't know *that* you are here.
(4) Exists only in plural form.
(5) The combination *noch nicht* means *not yet*.
(6) The latter functions as a relative pronoun.

GERMAN - ENGLISH
DICTIONARY

A

ab from, from ~ on
Abend *m* **der** evening
Abendessen *n* **das** dinner
abends in the evening
aber but
Abfall *m* **der** waste
Abflug *m* **der** take-off, departure (of a plane)
Abreise *f* **die** departure
Abschluß *m* **der** conclusion; settlement
absichtlich deliberate
Adjektiv *n* **das** adjective
Adresse *f* **die** address
Adverb *n* **das** adverb
ähnlich similar
Ähnlichkeit *f* **die** similarity
alle all, every
allein alone; **von alleine** by himself, by herself
alles everything
allgemein general, generally; **im Allgemeinen**
    in general
alltäglich daily, common
allzu too
Alpen *f/pl.* **die** Alps
als as, like; than; when; **als ob** as if
also thus, therefore
alt old
am = an dem
Ameise *f* **die** ant
Amt *n* **das** office, agency; **Postamt** *n* **das** post office
an at, on, to

anbieten *V*1* offer

andere other

ändern *V* change

anders different, differently, otherwise

Anfang *m* **der** beginning

anfangen *V*1* begin, start

anfassen *V1* touch

Angebot *n* **das** offer

Angewohnheit *f* **die** habit

angreifen *V*1* attack

Angriff *m* **der** attack

Angst *f* **die** fear, anxiety

ankommen *V*1* arrive

Ankunft *f* **die** arrival

anmelden *V1* announce; enroll for, apply for

Anmeldung *f* **die** application

Anruf *m* **der** call, phone call

anrufen *V1* call, phone

anschauen *V1* watch, look at

ansehen *V*1* watch, look at

anstatt instead (of)

Antenne *f* **die** antenna

Antwort *f* **die** answer

antworten *V* answer

Anwalt *m* **der** advocate

Anzug *m* **der** dress, clothing; (men's) suit

Apfel *m* **der** apple

Apotheke *f* **die** pharmacy

Apparat *m* **der** apparatus, instrument

Appetit *m* **der** appetite; **Guten Appetit!** Bon
   appétit!

April *m* **der** April

Arbeit *f* **die** work

arbeiten *V* work

Arbeitsplatz *m* **der** job

Arbeitszeit *f* **die** working hours

Ärger *m* **der** anger, annoyance

ärgern *V* irritate, make angry; **sich ärgern** feel angry, get angry

arm poor

Arm *m* **der** arm, hand

Arsch *m* **der** ass (*vulgar*)

Art *f* **die** way, sort, kind

Arzt *m* **der** doctor

Atem *m* **der** breath

atmen *V* breath

auch also, too; **auch nicht** neither

auf on; open; **Auf Wiedersehen!** Good-bye!

Aufenthalt *m* **der** stay, sojourn

Aufenthaltsgenehmigung *f* **die** residence permit

Aufgabe *f* **die** task, job

aufstehen *V*1* stand up; get up

Auftrag *m* **der** commission; mission

aufwachen *V1* awake, wake up

aufwecken *V1* wake up

Auge *n* **das** eye

August *m* **der** August

aus out, out of; from; off

Ausfahrt *f* **die** excursion; exit

Ausflug *m* **der** excursion, trip

Ausfuhr *f* **die** export

Ausgabe *f* **die** expense; edition (of a book)

ausgeben *V*1* spend

ausgehen *V*1* go out; end

Ausland *n* **das** foreign country

Ausländer *m* **der** foreigner

Auslandsgespräch *n* **das** international call

Auslandsreise *f* **die** trip abroad

Ausnahme *f* **die** exception

ausruhen (sich) *V1* rest

ausschalten *V1* switch off

aussehen *V*1* look

aus Versehen by mistake
außen outside, out
außer except, besides; **außer daß** except that;
    außer wenn unless
Aussprache *f* **die** pronunciation
aussprechen *V*1* pronounce
Ausrüstung *f* **die** equipment
aussuchen *V1* choose
Ausweis *m* **der** identity card, passport
Auto *n* **das** car
Autobahn *f* **die** highway
Autobus *m* **der** bus, autobus
Autor *m* **der** author, writer
Autovermietung *f* **die** car rental

B

Baby *n* **das** baby
backen *V** bake
Bäcker *m* **der** baker
Bäckerei *f* **die** bakery
Bad *n* **das** bath; bathroom
baden *V* bath, take a bath
Bahnhof *m* **der** railway station, station
Bakterie *f* **die** germ, bacterium
bald soon
Balkon *m* **der** balcony
Band *n* **das** band, ribbon
Band *m* **der** volume
Bank *f* **die** bank
bar cash, in cash
Bar *f* **die** bar, pub
Bargeld *n* **das** cash
Bart *m* **der** beard
Bauch *m* **der** belly
bauen *V* build

Bauer *m* **der** farmer
Baum *m* **der** tree
Baumwolle *f* **die** cotton
beachten *V2* observe, note, notice, consider
Beamte *m* **der** public servant, officer
bedauern *V2* be sorry, regret
bedeuten *V2* mean, signify
Bedienung *f* **die** service
Beere *f* **die** berry
begleiten *V2* accompany
Begleitung *f* **die** company
behindern *V2* hinder
behindert handicapped (physically or mentally)
Behinderte *m/f* **der/die** handicapped person
Behinderung *f* **die** handicap
bei by, at, near, with
beide, beides both
Beilage *f* **die** side dish
Bein *n* **das** leg, foot
Beispiel *n* **das** example
beißen *V** bite
bekannt known, well-known
beklagen (sich) *V2* complain
bekommen *V*2* get, receive
belegt occupied, reserved; busy (tel.)
beliebt popular
bemerken *V2* notice
benehmen (sich) *V*2* behave
benutzen *V2* use
Benzin *n* **das** gas, gasoline
beobachten *V2* observe, watch
bequem comfortable, convenient
berauben *V2* rob
bereit ready
Berg *m* **der** mountain, hill

Bergbahn *f* **die** mountain-railway, cable car, cable railway

Beruf *m* **der** profession, job

beruhigen *V2* calm, calm down

berühmt famous

berühren *V2* touch

bescheiden modest

beschreiben *V*2* describe

beschützen *V* protect, guard

Beschwerde *f* **die** complaint

beschweren (sich) *V2* complain

besichtigen *V2* view, visit (e.g. a tourist attraction)

Besitz *m* **der** possession

besitzen *V*2* possess, own

besonders special, especially

besorgt worried

besser better

Beste *m/f* **der/die** best; **am besten** best

bestechen *V*2* bribe

Besteck *n* **das** knife, fork, and spoon

bestellen *V* order

Bestellung *f* **die** order

bestimmt surely

Besuch *m* **der** visit

besuchen *V2* visit

Betrug *m* **der** cheat, fraud

betrügen *V*2* cheat

betrunken drunk, drunken

Bett *n* **das** bed

betteln *V* beg

Bettler *m* **der** beggar

bevor before

bewegen *V2* move

Beweis *m* **der** proof, evidence

bewohnen *V2* inhabit, live in

bewußt conscious, deliberate

bezahlen *V2* pay
Bezahlung *f* **die** payment
Bezirk *m* **der** district, region
Bibel *f* **die** bible
Bier *n* **das** beer
Biergarten *m* **der** beer garden
Bild *n* **das** picture
billig cheap
Birne *f* **die** pear; lightbulb
bis to, up to, as far as, until, till
bißchen, ein bit, little bit
bitte please; **bitte sehr!, bitte schön!** please!
Bitte! (You're) welcome!
Bitte *f* **die** request
bitten *V** ask (for), request
bitter bitter
Blase *f* **die** bladder
Blatt *n* **das** leaf; sheet (of paper); **ein Blatt
    Papier** a piece of paper
blau blue
bleiben *V** stay, remain
Bleistift *m* **der** pencil
blind blind
Blitz *m* **der** lightning
blöd stupid
blond blond
bloß only, just
Blume *f* **die** flower
Blumenstraß *m* **der** bunch of flowers
Blut *n* **das** blood
bluten *V* bleed
Boden *m* **der** floor, soil
Bohne *f* **die** bean
Bonbon *n* **das** bonbon, sweet
Boot *n* **das** boat
Börse *f* **die** Stock Exchange; purse

böse mean, evil, bad
Boutique *f* **die** boutique
Branche *f* **die** industrial sector
braten *V** roast, grill
Brauch *m* **der** custom, use
brauchen *V* need
braun brown
Braut *f* **die** bride
Bräutigam *m* **der** groom
breit broad, large
Bremse *f* **die** break
bremsen *V* break
brennen *V** burn
Brief *m* **der** letter
Briefkasten *m* **der** mailbox
Briefmarke *f* **die** stamp
Briefumschlag *m* **der** envelope
Brille *f* **die** glasses
bringen *V** bring, take
Brot *n* **das** bread
Brötchen *n* **das** roll
Brücke *f* **die** bridge
Bruder *m* **der** brother
Brust *f* **die** breast
brutal brutal
brutto gross
Buch *n* **das** book
buchen *V* book
Buchstabe *m* **der** letter
Budget *n* **das** budget
Buffet *n* **das** buffet, counter
Bühne *f* **die** stage
Burg *f* **die** castle, citadel
Bürger *m* **der** citizen
Büro *n* **das** office
Bürste *f* **die** brush

Bus *m* **der** bus
Busch *m* **der** bush
Butter *f* **die** butter

C

Café *n* **das** bar, café
Celsius degree centigrade, Celsius
Champignon *m* **der** mushroom
Charakter *m* **der** character
Chor *m* **der** choir
circa about, circa, approximately

D

da there, here; because, since, as
Dach *n* **das** roof
dafür for that; in return; instead of it (something
  mentioned before)
dagegen against that (something mentioned before)
daheim at home
daher therefore, hence; from there
dahin there, to there
dahinter behind it
damals then, at that time
Dame *f* **die** lady
damit so that, in order to; with it, with that
danach after this, afterwards
Dank *m* **der** thanks, gratitude
danke thanks, thank you
dann then
Darm *m* **der** gut, intestines
das *art.* the
daß that
Datum *n* **das** date
Dauer *f* **die** duration
Daumen *m* **der** thumb
davon from this/that, about this/that

Decke _f_ **die** cover, blanket
dein your, yours
delikat delicate; delicious
dem _art._ to the
denken _V*_ think
denn because, for, since; than
Deodorant _n_ **das** deodorant
der _art._ the
des _art._ of the
desto: je ..., desto ... the ..., the ...
Dezember _m_ **der** December
Diabetiker _m_ **der** diabetic
Dialekt _m_ **der** dialect
Diät _f_ **die** diet
dich you, yourself
dick thick, big
die _art._ the
Dieb _m_ **der** thief
Dienstag _m_ **der** Tuesday
Diesel _n_ **das** diesel
Ding _n_ **das** thing
Diplomat _m_ **der** diplomat
diplomatisch diplomatic
direkt direct
Direktor _m_ **der** director, principal
Diskette _f_ **die** floppy disk; disk
Diskussion _f_ **die** discussion
diskutieren discuss
doch but, yet, however
Doktor _m_ **der** doctor
Donner _m_ **der** thunder
Donnerstag _m_ **der** Thursday
doof silly, stupid
doppelt double; **doppelt so viel** twice as much
Dorf _n_ **das** village
dort there, over there

Dose *f* **die** can
Dosenöffner *m* **der** can opener
Drama *n* **das** drama
draußen outside
Dreck *m* **der** dirt, mud
drehen *V* turn
dringend urgent
drinnen inside
Drogerie *f* **die** drugstore
Druck *m* **der** pressure
drücken *V* press, push
du you; **du selber** you yourself
Duft *m* **der** scent, smell, fragrance
dumm stupid, dumb
dunkel dark, gloomy
Dunkelheit *f* **die** darkness
dünn thin
durch through, by
durcheinander mixed up, in a jumble
Durchfall *m* **der** diarrhea
Durchreise *f* **die** transit
Durchsage *f* **die** announcement
Durchschnitt *m* **der** average
durchschnittlich average
Durchwahl *f* **die** (tel.) direct dialing, extension
  number
dürfen *V** be allowed, be permitted
Durst *m* **der** thirst
durstig thirsty
Dusche *f* **die** shower
duschen *V* take a shower

E
Ebbe *f* **die** low tide, ebb tide
echt real, genuine
Ecke *f* **die** corner

edel noble

Ehe *f* **die** marriage

Ehefrau *f* **die** wife

Ehemann *m* **der** husband

Ehre *f* **die** honor

ehrlich honest, sincere

Ei *n* **das** egg

Eiche *f* **die** oak

eigen own, separate, individual

eigentlich actually

Eile *f* **die** haste, hurry

eilig hasty, in a hurry

Eimer *m* **der** bucket

ein *art.* a

einbrechen *V*1* break in, burglarize

Einbrecher *m* **der** burglar

Eindruck *m* **der** impression

einfach single, simple, plain

Einfuhr *f* **die** import

einführen *V1* introduce

Einführung *f* **die** introduction, initiation

eingebildet conceited

Eingeweide *n/pl.* **die** viscera, bowels

einig united

einige some, a few

Einkauf *m* **der** purchase

einkaufen *V1* buy (things), go shopping

Einkommen *n* **das** income

Einkommensteuer *f* **die** income tax

Einleitung *f* **die** introduction

einmal once

Einreise *f* **die** entry

einrichten *V1* install, furnish, arrange

Einrichtung *f* **die** equipment, installation;
    establishment, institution

einschenken *V1* pour out, pour in

einschließen *V*1* lock, lock up
Einwanderer *m* **der** immigrant
Einwohner *m* **der** inhabitant
Einzahl *f* **die** singular
einzeln single
einzig only, sole, single
Eis *n* **das** ice; ice cream
Eisen *n* **das** iron
Eisenbahn *f* **die** railroad
Eiweiß *n* **das** protein; egg white
Ekel *m* **der** disgust, nausea
eklig disgusting
elektrisch electric, electrical
elektronisch electronic
Eltern *pl.* **die** parents
Emanzipation *f* **die** emancipation
Empfang *m* **der** reception
Empfänger *m* **der** receiver
Empfängnisverhütung *f* **die** contraception
empfindlich sensitive
Ende *n* **das** end
enden *V* terminate, end
endlich finally
Endung *f* **die** ending
Energie *f* **die** energy
eng narrow
Enge *f* **die** narrowness; tightness
Engel *m* **der** angel
englisch English
Enkel *m* **der** grandchild
entlassen *V*2* dismiss
entscheiden *V*2* decide
Entscheidung *f* **die** decision
entschieden decided, determined
entschuldigen *V2* excuse, apologize
Entschuldigung *f* **die** excuse, apology

Entschuldigung! Sorry!

entspannen *V2* relax

Entspannung *f* **die** relaxation

enttäuschen *V2* disappoint

Enttäuschung *f* **die** disappointment

entweder ... oder ... or ... or ...

er he

Erbe *n* **das** heritage

erben *V* inherit

erbrechen *V*2* vomit, throw up

Erdbeere *f* **die** strawberry

Erde *f* **die** earth; soil

Erdgeschoß *n* **das** first floor

Erdöl *n* **das** mineral oil, petrol

erfinden *V*2* invent

Erfolg *m* **der** success

Ergebnis *n* **das** result

erholen (sich) *V2* recover

Erholung *f* **die** recovery

erinnern (sich) *V2* remember

Erinnerung *f* **die** remembrance, recollection

erkennen *V*2* recognize, perceive

erklären *V2* explain

Erklärung *f* **die** explanation

erlauben *V2* permit, allow

Erlaubnis *f* **die** permission

ernähren *V2* feed, nourish

Ernährung *f* **die** nutrition

ernst serious

ernsthaft serious

Ernte *f* **die** harvest

erraten *V*2* guess

erschaffen *V*2* create

erschrecken *V*2* frighten, scare

ersetzen *V2* replace

erst only

erste, erster, erstes first
erwachsen adult, grown-up
erwarten *V2* expect, await
erzählen *V2* tell
erziehen *V*2* educate
Erziehung *f* **die** education
es it
Eßbesteck *n* **das** knife, fork and spoon
essen *V*** eat
Essen *n* **das** food; meal
etwa about, approximately
etwas something
euch *pl.* you, to you; yourselves
euer *pl.* your, of you; yours
Europa Europe
Europäer/Europäerin *m/f* **der/die** European
europäisch European
Euroscheck *m* **der** Eurocheque (European check)
ewig eternal
Examen *n* **das** exam, examination (school)
exklusiv exclusive
Experiment *n* **das** experiment
Export *m* **der** export
expreß express
extra, extra- especially, extra-

F

Fabrik *f* **die** factory
Fach *n* **das** subject; shelf
faden *m* **der** thread
fähig able, skilled, competent
Fahne *f* **die** flag, banner
fahren *V*** go, ride, drive
Fahrer *m* **der** driver
Fahrkarte *f* **die** ticket
Fahrkartenschalter *m* **der** ticket office

Fahrplan *m* **der** timetable
Fahrpreis *m* **der** fare
Fahrrad *n* **das** bicycle, bike
Fahrt *f* **die** journey; ride
Fall *m* **der** case; fall
fallen *V** fall
falsch wrong, false
Falschgeld *n* **das** counterfeit money
Fälschung *f* **die** falsification, fake
familiär familiar
Familie *f* **die** family
Familienname *m* **der** last name, surname
Fantasie *f* **die** fantasy
fantastisch fantastic
Farbe *f* **die** color
Faß *n* **das** barrel, cask
fassen *V* get, seize, hold
fast almost, nearly
faul lazy; rotten
Fax *n* **das** fax
Faxgerät *n* **das** fax machine
Februar *m* **der** February
Feder *f* **die** feather
fehlen *V* be absent, be missing
Fehler *m* **der** mistake; defect
fehlerfrei faultless
Feier *f* **die** celebration
fein fine, subtle, delicate
Feind/Feindin *m/f* **der/die** enemy
feindlich hostile
Feld *n* **das** field, ground
Fell *n* **das** fur, pelt
Fels *m* **der** rock
Fenster *n* **das** window
Ferien *pl.* **die** vacation, holidays
Ferienwohnung *f* **die** holiday flat

Ferienzeit *f* **die** holiday season
Ferngespräch *n* **das** long-distance call
Fernseher *m* **der** television
fertig ready, finished
fest firm, solid
Fest *n* **das** festivity, party
fett fat, big
Fett *n* **das** fat
fettig fat, greasy
feucht moist, humid
Feuchtigkeit *f* **die** humidity
Feuer *n* **das** fire
Feueralarm *m* **der** fire alarm
Feuerlöscher *m* **der** fire extinguisher
Feuerwehr *f* **die** fire department
Feuerwerk *n* **das** fireworks
Feuerzeug *n* **das** lighter
Fieber *n* **das** fever
Filet *n* **das** fillet
Film *m* **der** movie; film
Filter *m* **der** filter
Finanzamt *n* **das** revenue office
finden *V** find
Finger *m* **der** finger
Firma *f* **die** firm, company
Fisch *m* **der** fish
flach flat, plain; shallow
Fläche *f* **die** surface, plane
Flamme *f* **die** flame
Flasche *f* **die** bottle
Fleisch *n* **das** meat
fleißig diligent, painstaking
Fliege *f* **die** fly
fliegen *V** fly
fliehen *V** flee
fließen *V** flow

flirten *V* flirt

Fluch *m* **der** swearword; curse

fluchen *V* swear; curse

Flucht *f* **die** escape

Flug *m* **der** flight

Fluß *m* **der** river

flüssig liquid, fluid

Flut *f* **die** flood, high tide

folgen *V* follow, succeed

Fön *m* **der** hair dryer

fordern *V* demand, ask, require

Form *f* **die** form, shape

forschen *V* search, inquire

Forscher *m* **der** researcher, scientist

fort away; gone

fortfahren *V*1* go away; continue

fortgehen *V*1* go away

Fortsetzung *f* **die** continuation, pursuit

Foto *n* **das** photograph, picture

Fracht *f* **die** freight, load

Frage *f* **die** question, inquiry

fragen *V* ask

Frau *f* **die** woman; **Frau ...** (followed by a name) Mrs. ...

frei free; independent; vacant

Freiheit *f* **die** freedom, liberty

Freistaat *m* **der** free state; **Freistaat Bayern** Free State of Bavaria

Freitag *m* **der** Friday

Freizeit *f* **die** leisure time, spare time

Freizeitkleidung *f* **die** leisure wear

fremd foreign, strange

fremdartig strange, odd

Fremde *f* **die** stranger, foreigner

Fremder *m* **der** stranger, foreigner

Freude *f* **die** joy, happiness, gladness

freuen (sich) be happy
Freund *m* **der** friend, boyfriend
Freundin *f* **die** friend, girlfriend
Frieden *m* **der** peace
friedlich peaceful
frisch fresh
Friseur *m* **der** hairdresser
Frisur *f* **die** hairstyle
Frucht *f* **die** fruit
früh early, in the morning
Frühling *m* **der** spring
Frühstück *n* **das** breakfast
fühlen *V* feel
führen *V* guide, lead
Führer *m* **der** guide, leader
funktionieren *V2* work, function
für for, by
Furcht *f* **die** fear
für immer forever
Fürst *m* **der** sovereign, prince
Fuß *m* **der** foot, leg
Fußball *m* **der** soccer
Futur *n* **das** future tense

G

Gabel *f* **die** fork
ganz whole, entire; all
gar well-cooked, done
Garantie *f* **die** guarantee, warranty
garantieren *V2* guarantee, warrant
Garten *m* **der** garden
Gas *n* **das** gas
Gast *m* **der** guest, visitor
geben *V** give
Gebirge *n* **das** mountains
geboren born; **geboren werden** *V** be born

gebraten roasted

gebrauchen use

Gebrauchsanweisung *f* **die** directions for use

Geburt *f* **die** birth

Geburtsort *m* **der** birthplace

Geburtstag *m* **der** birthday

Gedächtnis *n* **das** memory, remembrance

Gedanke *m* **der** thought

Geduld *f* **die** patience

geduldig patient

Gefahr *f* **die** danger

gefährlich dangerous

gefallen *V**2 like, please

Gefallen *m* **der** favor

Gefängnis *n* **das** prison

Gefühl *n* **das** feeling, sensation; touch

gegen against; towards

Gegend *f* **die** region, area

gegeneinander against each other

Gegenmittel *n* **das** remedy, antidote

Gegenstand *m* **der** object, topic

Gegenteil *n* **das** contrary

gegenüber vis-à-vis, opposite side of

Gegner *m* **der** opponent

Gehalt *n* **das** salary; content

geheim secret

Geheimnis *n* **das** secret, mystery

gehen *V** go, walk, leave; **Wie geht es dir?** How are you?; **Das geht nicht!** That's not possible!

Gehirn *n* **das** brain

gehören *V* belong

Geige *f* **die** violin

geistig intellectual, mental

geistlich spiritual, religious

gelb yellow

Geld *n* **das** money; **Geld wechseln** *V* change money

Geldbeutel *m* **der** purse
Geldgeschäfte *n/pl.* **die** monetary transactions
Geldschein *m* **der** bill, banknote
Geldstück *n* **das** coin
Gelegenheit *f* **die** occasion
gelingen *V*2* succeed
gelten *V** be valid; have influence
gemein mean
Gemeinde *f* **die** community; congregation
gemeinsam together; common
gemischt mixed
gemütlich comfortable, cozy
genau exact
Generation *f* **die** generation
genial ingenious, brilliant
genug enough
genügen *V2* be enough
geöffnet open
gerade straight, even; just
geradeaus straight ahead, straight forward
geradeeben just now
Gerät *n* **das** tool, device
Geräusch *n* **das** sound
gerecht just, fair
Gericht *n* **das** dish, course; court (of justice)
gering small, little, slight
gern(e) gladly, with pleasure
Geruch *m* **der** smell, odor, scent
gesamt whole, entire
Geschäft *n* **das** business, affair; shop
geschäftlich on business, business
Geschäftsführer *m* **der** manager
Geschäftsmann *m* **der** businessman
Geschäftsreise *f* **die** business trip
Geschäftsreisende *m* **der** traveling salesman
Geschäftsviertel *n* **das** business district, downtown

geschehen V*2 happen
Geschenk n **das** present, gift
Geschichte f **die** history; story, tale
geschieden divorced
Geschirr n **das** tableware, vessel
geschlossen closed
Geschmack m **der** taste; flavor
Geschwindigkeit f **die** speed
Gesellschaft f **die** society; company
Gesetz n **das** law, statute
Gesicht n **das** face
Gespräch n **das** conversation, talk
gestatten V2 allow, permit; **Gestatten Sie?** May
    I? With your permission?
gestern yesterday
gesund healthy
Gesundheit f **die** health
Getränk n **das** drink, beverage
Getreide n **das** grain
Getriebe n **das** transmission; gears
Gewalt f **die** violence, power
Gewicht n **das** weight
gewinnen V*2 win
Gewitter n **das** thunderstorm
Gewohnheit f **die** habit, custom
gewöhnlich common, ordinary
gewohnt habitual
Gewürz n **das** spice, condiment
giftig poisonous
Gitarre f **die** guitar
glänzen V shine, glitter
Glas n **das** glass
glatt smooth; even
glauben V believe; think
gleich equal, alike
gleiche same, the same

gleichfalls likewise

Gleichgewicht *n* **das** balance, equilibrium

gleichzeitig at the same time, simultaneously

Gleis *n* **das** platform

Glück *n* **das** luck, fortune; happiness

glücklich lucky; happy

Glühbirne *f* **die** lightbulb

Gold *n* **das** gold

golden golden

Gott *m* **der** god

Grad *m* **der** degree, grade

Gramm *n* **das** gram

Grammatik *f* **die** grammar

Gräte *f* **die** fishbone

gratis gratis, free

Grenze *f* **die** border

Grenzübergang *m* **der** border crossing

grillen *V* grill, barbecue

groß great, tall, large

großartig great, magnificent, splendid

Größe *f* **die** size, height

Großhandel *m* **der** wholesale trade

grün green

Grund *m* **der** reason, motive; ground, soil

Gruß *m* **der** greeting, salutation

grüßen *V* greet, say hello

gültig valid

Gürtel *m* **der** belt

gut good, well

Gute Nacht! Good night!

Guten Appetit! Bon appétit!

Guten Morgen! Good morning!

Gymnasium *n* **das** secondary school (10/11 to 18/19 yrs.)

Gymnastik *f* **die** gymnastics

H

Haar *n* **das** hair
haben *V* have
Hafen *m* **der** harbor
Hahn *m* **der** rooster; faucet
Haken *m* **der** hook
halb half
Halbinsel *f* **die** peninsula
Halbkugel *f* **die** hemisphere
hallo hello
Hals *m* **der** neck, throat
Halt *m* **der** stop
halten *V** hold, keep
Hand *f* **die** hand
Handel *m* **der** trade, commerce
handeln *V* trade; act
Handelsverkehr *m* **der** trade traffic
Handelsvertrag *m* **der** commercial treaty
Handlung *f* **die** action; store
Handtuch *n* **das** towel
Hardware *f* **die** hardware
harmlos harmless
hart hard
Härte *f* **die** hardness
hassen *V* hate
Haupt *n* **das** head, chief; **Haupt-** (as prefix) head,
    main, principal
Haus *n* **das** house, home
Haut *f* **die** skin
heben *V** lift, raise
Hefe *f* **die** yeast
heftig vehement, violent
heilen *V* cure, heal
heilig sacred, holy
Heimat *f* **die** home, native country
heiraten *V* marry

heiß hot

heißen *V** be called, be named

Held *m* **der** hero

helfen *V** help

hell bright

Hemd *m* **das** shirt

her to, towards (a place/object)

heraus out of

Herbst *m* **der** fall

herein into; **Herein!** Come in!

Herr *m* **der** sir, mister; **Herr ...** (followed by a name) Mr. ...

herunter down

Herz *n* **das** heart

heute today

Hexe *f* **die** witch

hier here

hierher, hierhin here

Hilfe *f* **die** help

Himmel *m* **der** sky, heaven

hin there, to (a place/object)

hinaus out

hinein into

hinten behind

hinter behind of

hinüber across

Hitze *f* **die** heat

hoch high

Hochdeutsch *n* **das** High German

Hochzeit *f* **die** wedding, marriage

Hof *m* **der** courtyard; farm

hoffen *V* hope

Hoffnung *f* **die** hope

höflich polite

Höhe *f* **die** height

höher higher

Höhle *f* **die** cave
holen *V* fetch, get
Holz *n* **das** wood
Holzkohle *f* **die** charcoal
hören *V* hear, listen
Hose *f* **die** trousers, pants
Hospital *n* **das** hospital
Hotel *n* **das** hotel
hübsch pretty
Hügel *m* **der** hill
Huhn *n* **das** chicken
Hund *m* **der** dog
Hunger *m* **der** hunger
hungrig hungry
husten *V* cough
Husten *m* **der** cough
Hütte *f* **die** shack

I

ich I
Idee *f* **die** idea
ihr *pl.* you; your (polite)
illegal illegal
im = **in dem**
immer always; **für immer** forever
Imperfekt *n* **das** past tense
im voraus in advance
in in; into; within
Industrie *f* **die** industry
Industriegebiet *n* **das** industrial area
Inhaber *m* **der** owner
Inhalt *m* **der** contents
Injektion *f* **die** injection
innen within, inside, in
Insekt *n* **das** insect
Insel *f* **die** island

Institution *f* **die** institution
Instrument *n* **das** instrument; tool
interessant interesting
interessieren (sich) *V2* be interested in
irgend, irgendein some, any
irgendjemand someone
irgendwann some time
irgendwie somehow
irgendwo somewhere

J

ja yes
Jacke *f* **die** jacket
Jahr *n* **das** year
Jahrgang *m* **der** vintage, year
Januar *m* **der** January
je ..., desto ... the ..., the ...
jede *f* every, everybody, everyone
jeder *m* every, everybody, everyone
jedes *n* every, everybody, everyone
jemand somebody, someone
Jude *m* **der** Jew
jüdisch Jewish
Jugend *f* **die** youth
Juli *m* **der** July
jung young
Junge *m* **der** boy
Juni *m* **der** June
Jurist *m* **der** lawyer, jurist
Justiz *f* **die** justice

K

Kabel *n* **das** cable
Kabine *f* **die** cabin
Käfer *m* **der** bug, beetle
Kaffee *m* **der** coffee

Kakerlake *f* **die** cockroach
Kalb *n* **das** calf
Kalbfleisch *n* **das** veal
kalt cold
Kamera *f* **die** camera
Kamm *m* **der** comb
Kampf *m* **der** fight, battle
kämpfen *V* fight
Kanal *m* **der** channel
kann, kannst → **können**
Kanzler *m* **der** chancellor
kapieren *V2* understand, get it
kaputt broken
Karte *f* **die** card; map
Kartoffel *f* **die** potato
Käse *m* **der** cheese
Kasse *f* **die** cashier, cash register
Kassette *f* **die** cassette
Kater *m* **der** tomcat; hangover
Katze *f* **die** cat
kaufen *V* buy
Kaufhaus *n* **das** shopping center, shopping mall, mall
Kaufmann *m* **der** merchant, businessman, dealer
Kehle *f* **die** throat
kein no, not any, none
keiner nobody, no one
Keks *m* **der** cookie, cracker
Kellner *m* **der** waiter
Kellnerin *f* **die** waitress
kennen *V** know
Kerl *m* **der** guy, fellow
Kern *m* **der** kernel, pit
Kerze *f* **die** candle
Kette *f* **die** chain
Kilo, Kilogramm *n* **das** kilogram
Kilometer *m* **der** kilometer

Kind *n* **das** child
Kinderarzt *m* **der** pediatrician
Kindergarten *m* **der** kindergarten
Kindertagesstätte *f* **die** day-care center
Kino *n* **das** cinema, movie theater
Kirche *f* **die** church
Kirchturm *m* **der** church tower
kitzeln *V* tickle
Klage *f* **die** complaint; lawsuit
klagen *V* complain; sue
klar clear; obvious
Klasse *f* **die** class; grade
klassisch classic
klauen *V* steal, pinch
Klavier *n* **das** piano
Kleid *n* **das** dress
kleiden *V* dress
Kleidung *f* **die** clothing, clothes
klein small, little
Klima *n* **das** climate
klingen *V** sound
klingeln *V* ring
Klischee *n* **das** cliché
Klo, Klosett *n* **das** toilet, lavatory
klopfen *V* knock
Kloster *n* **das** cloister
klug clever, intelligent, smart
Knall *m* **der** bang
Kneipe *f* **die** bar, saloon
Knie *n* **das** knee
Knochen *m* **der** bone
Knopf *m* **der** button
Koch *m* **der** cook
kochen *V* cook
Koffer *m* **der** suitcase
Kohl *m* **der** cabbage

Kohle *f* **die** coal, charcoal
Kollege *m* **der** colleague
Kombination *f* **die** combination
komisch funny, comic
kommen *V** come, arrive
Kompliment *n* **das** compliment
Komponist *m* **der** composer
Konditorei *f* **die** pastry shop
Konferenz *f* **die** conference
König *m* **der** king
Konkurrenz *f* **die** competition
können *V** be able, know, understand
Kontakt *m* **der** contact
Kontrolle *f* **die** check, supervision
kontrollieren *V2* check, verify, control
Konversation *f* **die** conversation
Kopf *m* **der** head; top; brain
Kopie *f* **die** copy, duplicate
kopieren *V2* copy
Korb *m* **der** basket; refusal
Korn *n* **das** grain
Körper *m* **der** body
korrekt correct, right
kosten *V* cost; taste
Kraft *f* **die** power; strength
kräftig strong, powerful
Krampf *m* **der** cramp, spasm
krank sick, ill
Krankenhaus *n* **das** hospital
Krankenkasse *f* **die** health insurance, insurance
Krankenschwester *f* **die** nurse
Krankenwagen *m* **der** ambulance
Krankheit *f* **die** disease, sickness
Kraut *n* **das** herb; **Kräuter** *n/pl.* **die** herbs
Kreis *m* **der** circle
Kreuz *n* **das** cross

Kreuzung *f* **die** crossroads; crossing
Krieg *m* **der** war
Kritik *f* **die** criticism; review
kritisieren *V2* criticize
Krone *f* **die** crown
Krüppel *m* **der** cripple
Küche *f* **die** kitchen; cuisine
Kuchen *m* **der** cake
Küchenschabe *f* **die** cockroach
Kugel *f* **die** ball; bullet
Kuh *f* **die** cow
kühl cool, fresh, cold
Kühlschrank *m* **der** refrigerator, fridge
Kultur *f* **die** culture
kulturell cultural
Kümmel *m* **der** cumin
Kunde *m* **der** client
Kunst *f* **die** art
Künstler *m* **der** artist
künstlich artificial
Kur *f* **die** cure
Kurs *m* **der** rate, quotation; course, route
kurz short, brief
Kuß *m* **der** kiss
küssen *V* kiss

L

lächeln *V* smile
Lächeln *n* **das** smile
lachen *V* laugh
Lachs *m* **der** salmon
Laden *m* **der** shop
Lage *f* **die** situation; position
Lager *n* **das** camp; deposit
Lamm *n* **das** lamb
Land *n* **das** country, land, countryside

landen *V* land
Landkarte *f* **die** map
Landung *f* **die** landing
lang long
langsam slow
langweilig boring
Lärm *m* **der** noise
lassen *V** let; allow, permit; leave
laufen *V** run, walk
laut loud, noisy
leben *V* live
Leben *n* **das** life
Lebensgefahr *n* **die** danger to life
lebensgefährlich dangerous to live
Lebensmittel *n/pl.* **die** food
Lebensmittelgeschäft *n* **das** food store, grocery
lecken *V* lick
Leder *n* **das** leather
leer empty
legal legal
legen *V* put, lay
lehren *V* teach
Lehrer *m* **der** teacher
Leiche *f* **die** corpse
leicht easy; light
Leid *n* **das** sorrow
leiden suffer
Leidenschaft *n* **die** passion
leidenschaftlich passionate
leider unfortunately
leid: Es tut mir leid! I'm sorry!
leihen *V** borrow; lend, loan
leise soft, silent
Leitung *f* **die** direction, management; mains (pipes)
lernen *V* learn, study
lesen *V** read

letzte *f*, **letzer** *m*, **letztes** *n* last
Leute *pl.* **die** people
Lexikon *n* **das** dictionary, encyclopedia
Licht *n* **das** light
lieb nice, kind, dear
Liebe *f* **die** love
lieben *V* love
Lied *n* **das** song
liegen *V** lie, be
links left, on the left, to the left
loben *V* praise
Loch *n* **das** hole
locker relaxed; loose
Löffel *m* **der** spoon
los! go ahead!
Luft *f* **die** air
Lüftung *f* **die** ventilation
Lüge *f* **die** lie
lügen *V** lie
Lunge *f* **die** lung
Lust *f* **die** pleasure, delight; desire
lust haben *V* feel like
lustig funny

M

machen *V* make, do
Macht *f* **die** power, control, might
mächtig powerful, mighty
Mädchen *n* **das** girl
Magen *m* **der** stomach
Magenschmerzen *m/pl.* **die** stomachache
mager meager, lean; thin
Mai *m* **der** May
-mal times; **zweimal** twice; **zehnmal** ten times
malen *V* paint, draw

Maler *m* **der** painter, artist

man one, someone, people (*impersonal indefinite article*)

Mann *m* **der** man

männlich male, masculine

Mantel *m* **der** coat

März *m* **der** March

Maschine *f* **die** machine

Maß *n* **das** measure; (beer) quart, one liter

Material *n* **das** material

Mauer *f* **die** wall

Medikament *n* **das** medicine, drug, medication

Medizin *f* **die** medicine, medication

Meer *n* **das** sea, seaside, ocean

Mehl *n* **das** flour

mehr more; **nicht mehr** no more, no longer; **mehr als** more than

mehrfach multiple, repeated

mein my, mine

Meinung *f* **die** opinion

meist, meistens most, most often

melden *V* announce, report

Meldung *f* **die** announcement, report

Melodie *f* **die** melody

Menge *f* **die** amount, quantity, multitude

Mensch *m* **der** man, person

merken *V* notice, observe, feel

messen *V** measure

Messer *n* **das** knife

Metall *n* **das** metal

Meter *m* **der** meter

Methode *f* **die** method, way

Metzger *m* **der** butcher

Miete *f* **die** rent

mieten *V* rent, hire

Mietwagen *m* **der** hired car

Milch *f* **die** milk
Militär *n* **das** army
mindestens at least, minimum
Minister *m* **der** minister
Minute *f* **die** minute
mischen *V* mix; shuffle
Mission *f* **die** mission
mit with, by means of
mitbringen *V*1* bring, bring along
mitgehen *V*1* go along, go with, accompany
mitmachen *V1* join, follow
mitnehmen *V*1* take along, take away
Mittag *m* **der** noon
Mittagessen *n* **das** lunch
Mitte *f* **die** middle, center
mitteilen *V1* communicate, notify
mitten in the middle of
Mittwoch *m* **der** Wednesday
Möbel *n* **das** furniture
Mode *f* **die** fashion
modern modern
mögen *V** like; wish, want
möglich possible
Moment *m* **der** moment
Monat *m* **der** month
Monatsbinde *f* **die** sanitary napkin
Mond *m* **der** moon
Montag *m* **der** Monday
Moral *f* **die** moral
moralisch moral
Mord *m* **der** murder
Mörder *m* **der** murderer
morgen tomorrow
Morgen *m* **der** morning
Motor *m* **der** motor

Motorrad *n* **das** motorbike

Mücke *f* **die** mosquito

Müll *m* **der** garbage

Mund *m* **der** mouth

Münze *f* **die** coin

Musik *f* **die** music

Muskel *m* **der** muscle

müssen *V** must, have to

Mut *m* **der** courage

mutig courageous, brave

Mutter *f* **die** mother

N

nach after; towards; according to; **nach Hause** home

nachher after, afterwards, later

Nachmittag *m* **der** afternoon

Nachname *m* **der** surname

Nachricht *f* **die** notice, report

Nachrichten *f/pl.* **die** news

nachsehen *V*1* look after, check

nächster next

Nacht *f* **die** night

nachts by night, at night

nackt nude

Nadel *f* **die** needle

nahe close, close to

Nähe *f* **die** proximity; **in der Nähe** close by

Nahrung *f* **die** food

Name *m* **der** name

nämlich that is, namely

Nase *f* **die** nose

naß wet

national national

Natur *f* **die** nature

natürlich naturally
Nebel *m* **der** fog
neben beside, besides
nehmen *V** take
Neid *m* **der** envy
nein no
nennen *V** call, name
nett nice, dear
netto net
Netz *n* **das** net
neu new
Neujahr *n* **das** New Year's Day
nicht not
nichts nothing
nie, niemals never; **nie wieder** never again
niedrig low
niemand nobody
noch still, yet; **noch nicht** not yet
Norden *m* **der** north
nördlich north
Nordosten *m* **der** northeast
normalerweise normally
Norwesten *m* **der** northwest
Notarzt *m* **der** emergency doctor
Notfall *m* **der** emergency
nötig necessary, required
Notiz *f* **die** note, memo
notwendig necessary, required
November *m* **der** November
nüchtern sober; with an empty stomach
Null *f* **die** null, zero
Nummer *f* **die** number
nun now, at present
nur only, solely
Nuß *f* **die** nut, walnut

Nutzen *m* **der** use, benefit, profit
nutzen, nützen *V* be useful, be of use; use

O

ob whether, if
oben above, on top; upstairs
Obst *n* **das** fruit
Ochse *m* **der** ox
oder or
Ofen *m* **der** oven
offen open
öffentlich public
oft often
ohne without
Ohr *n* **das** ear
Ohrfeige *f* **die** slap (in the face)
Oktober *m* **der** October
Öl *n* **das** oil; petrol
Olive *f* **die** olive
Omnibus *m* **der** bus
Oper *f* **die** opera
Operation *f* **die** surgery, operation
orange orange
Orange *f* **die** orange
ordentlich tidy, clean
ordnen *V* put in order, arrange
Ordnung *f* **die** order; arrangement; rules
Organ *n* **das** organ
Organisation *f* **die** organization
organisieren *V2* organize
Organismus *m* **der** organism
Original *n* **das** original
Orkan *m* **der** hurricane
Ort *m* **der** place; city
Osten *m* **der** east
östlich east

P

paar some, couple of
Paar *n* **das** pair, couple
Päckchen *n* **das** small parcel
Paket *n* **das** parcel, packet
Panzer *m* **der** tank
Papier *n* **das** paper
Pappe *f* **die** pasteboard, cardboard
Paprika *f* **die** paprika, red pepper
Pärchen *n* **das** couple
Parfüm *n* **das** perfume
Park *m* **der** park
parken *V* park (a car)
Parkplatz *m* **der** parking, parking lot
Parkverbot *n* **das** no parking
Parlament *n* **das** parliament
Paß *m* **der** passport
Passagier *m* **der** passenger
passen *V* fit
passieren *V2* happen, take place; pass
Pause *f* **die** break, intermission
Pech *n* **das** bad luck
peinlich embarrassing
Pelz *m* **der** fur
Pension *f* **die** boardinghouse; pension
perfekt perfect
Perfekt *n* **das** perfect tense
Perle *f* **die** pearl
Person *f* **die** person
Personal *n* **das** staff, personnel
persönlich personally
Pfanne *f* **die** pan, frying pan
Pfarrer *m* **der** pastor
Pfeffer *m* **der** pepper
Pfeil *m* **der** arrow
Pferd *n* **das** horse

Pfirsich *m* **der** peach
Pflanze *f* **die** plant
Pflaume *f* **die** plum
Pflicht *f* **die** duty, obligation
Pfund *n* **das** pound
Phantasie *f* **die** fantasy
phantastisch fantastic
Photo *n* **das** photograph, picture
Pickel *m* **der** pimple; pick(axe)
Pilz *m* **der** mushroom
Pistole *f* **die** gun
Plan *m* **der** plan
Plastik *n* **das** plastic
Plastiktüte *f* **die** plastic bag
Platz *m* **der** place, space
Plätzchen *n* **das** cookie, cracker
Plombe *f* **die** tooth filling
plötzlich suddenly, all of a sudden
Plural *m* **der** plural
Plusquamperfekt *n* **das** pluperfect
Politik *f* **die** politics
Politiker *m* **der** politician
Polizei *f* **die** police
Polizist *m* **der** policeman
populär popular
Portion *f* **die** serving, portion
Porto *n* **das** postage
Position *f* **die** position
Post *f* **die** post, mail
Postamt *n* **das** post office
praktisch practical, handy
Präsens *n* **das** present tense
Präsident *m* **der** president
Präteritum *n* **das** past tense
Praxis *f* **die** consulting room; practice
Preis *m* **der** price, fare

Priester *m* **der** priest

privat private

Probe *f* **die** trial; rehearsal

probieren *V2* try

Programm *n* **das** program

prost! cheers!

Prostituierte *f* **die** prostitute

Prostitution *f* **die** prostitution

Protest *m* **der** protest

protestieren *V2* protest

Proviant *m* **der** supplies

Provinz *f* **die** province

Prozent *n* **das** percent

Prozeß *m* **der** process

Prüfung *f* **die** check, verification; exam, examination

Publikum *n* **das** audience, spectators

Pullover *m* **der** sweater, sweatshirt

Punkt *m* **der** point

putzen *V* clean

Q

Quark *m* **der** curds

Quartier *n* **das** lodging

Quelle *f* **die** source, spring

quer cross, transverse, lateral

R

Rad *n* **das** wheel

Radio *n* **das** radio

Rand *m* **der** edge

Rasen *m* **der** grass

Rasierapparat *m* **der** razor

rasieren (sich) *V2* shave

Rasierklinge *f* **die** razor blade

Rat *m* **der** advice
raten *V** guess; advise
Rauch *m* **der** smoke
rauchen *V* smoke
Raum *m* **der** room; space
Rausch *m* **der** drunkenness, intoxication; **einen Rausch haben** be drunk
reagieren *V2* react
Reaktion *f* **die** reaction
rechnen *V* calculate; count on
Rechnung *f* **die** bill; calculation
Recht *n* **das** right, law, privilege
recht right, just, correct
rechts right, on the right, to the right
Rechtsanwalt *m* **der** advocate
Rechtschreibung *f* **die** orthography
reden *V* speak
Regel *f* **die** rule
regelmäßig regular
Regen *m* **der** rain
Regierung *f* **die** government
Region *f* **die** region
regnen *V* rain
reich rich
Reifen *m* **der** tire
rein pure; clean
Reis *m* **der** rice
Reise *f* **die** journey, voyage, travel, tour
Reiseführer *m* **der** guide; guidebook
reisen travel
Reklame *f* **die** publicity
Religion *f* **die** religion
Rente *f* **die** pension
Reparatur *f* **die** repair
reparieren *V2* repair
Reportage *f* **die** coverage

Republik *f* **die** republic
Reserve *f* **die** reservation
reservieren *V2* reserve, book
Rest *m* **der** rest, remainder
Restaurant *n* **das** restaurant
retten *V* save, rescue
Rettung *f* **die** rescue, escape
Revolution *f* **die** revolution
Rezept *n* **das** recipe
richtig right, correct
Richtung *f* **die** direction
riechen *V** smell
Rind *n* **das** cow, ox
Rindfleisch *n* **das** beef
Ring *m* **der** ring
Risiko *n* **das** risk
Rock *m* **der** skirt
Roggen *m* **der** rye
roh raw
Rohr *n* **das** pipe, tube
Roman *m* **der** novel
romantisch romantic
röntgen *V* x-ray
Röntgenstrahl *m* **der** x-ray
rosa pink
Rose *f* **die** rose
rot red
Rückfahrkarte *f* **die** return ticket
Rückfahrt *f* **die** return
Rucksack *m* **der** backpack
rückwärts back, backwards
rufen *V** call
Ruhe *f* **die** rest; silence
ruhig quiet, calm
Rührei *n* **das** scrambled eggs
rühren *V* stir

rund round
Ruß *m* **der** soot

S

Sache *f* **die** thing; affair, matter
sachlich factual; relevant
Safe *m* **der** safe
Saft *m* **der** juice
sagen *V* say
Salat *m* **der** salad
Salbe *f* **die** ointment, salve
Salz *n* **das** salt
Salzstreuer *m* **der** saltshaker
Salzwasser *n* **das** salt water
Samen *m* **der** seed; sperm
Samstag *m* **der** Saturday
Sand *m* **der** sand
sanft soft, gentle
Satz *m* **der** sentence, phrase; clause
sauber clean; neat
sauer sour, acid
Sauerkraut *n* **das** sauerkraut
Sauna *f* **die** sauna
S-Bahn *f* **die** (Germany) metro, subway
schade! what a pity!
schaden *V* injure, harm, be prejudicial
schädlich harmful, injurious
schaffen *V** create, produce; manage, achieve
Schale *f* **die** bowl, cup; peel, shell
schalten *V* switch
Schalter *m* **der** switch; counter
Scham *f* **die** shame, modesty
schämen (sich) *V* be ashamed, feel ashamed
schamlos shameless
scharf sharp; keen; hot, spicy
Schatten *m* **der** shadow

schauen *V* look, see

Schaum *m* **der** foam; lather

Scheck *m* **der** check

Scheibe *f* **die** slice; disk

Scheidung *f* **die** divorce

scheinen *V** appear, seem; shine

Scheiße *f* **die** shit (*vulgar*)

schenken *V* give, make a present

Schere *f* **die** scissors

Scherz *m* **der** joke

Schi *m* **der** ski

schießen *V** shoot

Schiff *n* **das** ship, boat, vessel

Schild *n* **das** sign, door-plate

Schinken *m* **der** ham

schlachten *V* slaughter

Schlaf *m* **der** sleep

Schlafanzug *m* **der** pajamas

schlafen *V** sleep

Schlafwagen *m* **der** sleeper (train car)

Schlafzimmer *n* **das** bedroom

schlagen *V** hit; beat

Schlamm *m* **der** mud

Schlange *f* **die** snake

schlecht bad, evil

schließen *V** close, shut; lock

schlimm bad, evil

Schloß *n* **das** lock; castle

Schluck *m* **der** gulp, sip

Schlüssel *m* **der** key

schmal narrow

schmecken *V* taste

Schmerz *m* **der** pain

schmerzen *V* hurt

Schminke *f* **die** makeup, rouge

schminken (sich) *V* apply makeup

Schmuck *m* **der** jewelry
Schmutz *m* **der** dirt, filth, smut
schmutzig dirty, filthy
Schnake *f* **die** crane fly
Schnaps *m* **der** liquor
Schnee *m* **der** snow
Schneeball *m* **der** snowball
Schneeflocke *f* **die** snowflake
Schneider *m* **der** tailor
schneien *V* snow
schnell quick, fast
Schnellimbiß *m* **der** snack
schon already
schön beautiful, pretty
Schönheit *f* **die** beauty
Schrank *m* **der** closet
Schraube *f* **die** screw
Schreck *m* **der** shock, terror
Schrei *m* **der** cry, yell
schreiben *V** write
schreien *V** yell, shout, cry
Schrift *f* **die** writing; handwriting
Schritt *m* **der** step
Schuh *m* **der** shoe
Schuld *f* **die** obligation; guilt; (money) debt
schulden *V* owe
schuldig guilty
Schule *f* **die** school
Schüler *m* **der** pupil
Schülerin *f* **die** pupil
Schuppe *f* **die** scale
Schuppen *f/pl.* **die** dandruff
Schuß *m* **der** shot
Schuster *m* **der** shoemaker
schütteln *V* shake
Schutz *m* **der** protection

schützen *V* protect, guard

schwach weak

Schwäche *f* **die** weakness; weak point

Schwager *m* **der** brother-in-law

Schwägerin *f* **die** sister-in law

schwanger pregnant

Schwanz *m* **der** tail

schwarz black

schweigen *V** be silent

Schwein *n* **das** pig, hog

Schweinebraten *m* **der** roast pork

Schweinefleisch *n* **das** pork

Schweiß *m* **der** sweat

schwer heavy; hard, difficult

Schwerkraft *f* **die** gravity

Schwerpunkt *m* **der** center of gravity

Schwester *f* **die** sister; (in a hospital) nurse

schwierig difficult, hard

Schwimmbad *n* **das** swimming pool; public baths

Schwimmbecken *n* **das** swimming pool

schwimmen *V** swim

schwindelig dizzy, giddy

schwitzen *V* sweat

schwul gay

schwül sultry

See *m* **der** lake

See *f* **die** sea, ocean

Seele *f* **die** soul, mind

Segelboot *n* **das** sailboat

Segen *m* **der** blessing

segnen *V* bless

sehen *V** see

Sehne *f* **die** sinew

sehr very

Seide *f* **die** silk

Seife *f* **die** soap

Seil *n* **das** rope, cable
sein *V** be
sein his
seit since
Seite *f* **die** side; page
Selbe *n* **das** same
selber self, oneself, on its own, itself
selbst self; **ich selbst** myself; **er selbst** himself
selbständig independent, self-employed
selten seldom
Semmel *f* **die** roll
senden *V* broadcast
Senf *m* **der** mustard
Sensation *f* **die** sensation
sensibel sensitive
September *m* **der** September
seriös serious, trustworthy
setzen *V* put, sit, place; **sich setzen** *V* sit down,
    take place
sich *refl. pr.* myself, yourself, himself, herself, itself,
    ourselves, yourselves, themselves
sicher secure, safe
Sicherheit *f* **die** security, safety
sicherlich sure, surely
sie she; you (polite)
Sieg *m* **der** victory
siegen *V* win
Silbe *f* **die** syllable
Silber *n* **das** silver
singen *V** sing
Singular *m* **der** singular
Sinn *m* **der** sense
Sitte *f* **die** custom, habit
Situation *f* **die** situation
sitzen *V** sit
Sitzung *f* **die** conference

Skala *f* **die** scale
Smoking *m* **der** tuxedo
so so, thus; as; **so daß** so that; **so ein** such a; **So ein Pech!** Such a pity!
Socke *f* **die** sock
sofort immediately, instantly, at once
Software *f* **die** software
sogar even
Sohn *m* **der** son
solch such
Soldat *m* **der** soldier
sollen shall, must
Sommer *m* **der** summer
sonder- (as prefix) special, extra-
sondern but
Sonne *f* **die** sun
Sonnenaufgang *m* **der** sunrise
Sonnenbad *n* **das** sunbath
Sonnenuntergang *m* **der** sunset
Sonntag *m* **der** Sunday
sonst else
Sorge *f* **die** sorrow; care
sorgfältig careful
Soße *f* **die** sauce
soviel so much
soweit so far, as far as
sowieso in any case
sozial social
spannend exciting, thrilling
Spannung *f* **die** tension; voltage
sparen *V* save
sparsam saving
Spaß *m* **der** fun
spät late; **Wie spät ist es?** What's the time?
später later
spazieren *V2* walk

spazierengehen $V*1$ go for a walk
Spaziergang *m* **der** walk, stroll
Speck *m* **der** bacon; fat
Speichel *m* **der** spittle, saliva
Speise *f* **die** dish, food
Sperre *f* **die** blockade, barrier
Spiegel *m* **der** mirror
Spiel *n* **das** game
spielen V play
Spielfilm *m* **der** movie, motion picture
Spielkasino *n* **das** casino
Spielzeug *n* **das** toys
Spinne *f* **die** spider
Spital *n* **das** (Austria, Switzerland) hospital
spitz pointed
Spitze *f* **die** point, top
Sport *m* **der** sports
sportlich sporting, athletic
Sprache *f* **die** language
Spray *n* **das** spray
sprechen $V*$ speak
Sprichwort *n* **das** saying, proverb
springen $V*$ jump
Spritze *f* **die** syringe; injection
Spucke *f* **die** spittle, saliva
Staat *m* **der** state
stabil stable
Stachel *m* **der** sting
Stadt *f* **die** city
Stahl *m* **der** steel
Stall *m* **der** stable, shed
stark strong, powerful
Start *m* **der** start; take-off
Stau *m* **der** traffic jam, congestion
stechen $V*$ prick, sting, pierce
Steckdose *f* **die** socket

Stecker *m* **der** plug
stehen *V** stand
steif stiff
Steigung *f* **die** rise, gradient, grade
steil steep
Stein *m* **der** stone
Stelle *f* **die** place
stellen *V* put, place, set, adjust
Stellung *f* **die** position; employment, job
Stempel *m* **der** stamp
sterben *V** die
Stern *m* **der** star
Steuer *n* **das** steering wheel, rudder
Steuer *f* **die** tax
Stich *m* **der** prick, sting
Stiefel *m* **der** boot
Stift *m* **der** pen
Stiftung *f* **die** foundation, donation
Stil *m* **der** style
still calm, quiet
Stimme *f* **die** voice
Stimmung *f* **die** mood, atmosphere
stinken *V** stink
Stirn *f* **die** forehead
Stock *m* **der** stick
Stoff *m* **der** fabric; material
stören *V* disturb
Störung *f* **die** disturbance, trouble
Stoß *m* **der** push; pile, stack
stoßen *V** push, hit
strafbar punishable
Strafe *f* **die** penalty, punishment
Strand *m* **der** beach
Straße *f* **die** street, road, way
Straßenbahn *f* **die** tramway, trolley line

Strauß *m* **der** bunch, bouquet
Strecke *f* **die** stretch; distance
streicheln *V* caress
Streichholz *m* **das** match
Streik *m* **der** strike, walkout
Streit *m* **der** quarrel, dispute, fight
streiten *V** fight, quarrel, argue
Strich *m* **der** stroke, line
Stroh *n* **das** straw
Strohhalm *m* **der** drinking straw
Strom *m* **der** current, electricity; river
Stromleitung *f* **die** mains, circuit line
Stromspannung *f* **die** voltage
Strömung *f* **die** stream, current; trend
Stück *n* **das** piece
Student *m* **der** student
studieren *V2* study
Stufe *f* **die** step; degree
Stuhl *m* **der** chair
Stunde *f* **die** hour; lesson
Sturm *m* **der** storm
Sturz *m* **der** fall, plunge, crash
stürzen *V* fall, tumble
Substantiv *n* **das** substantive, noun
Suche *f* **die** search, research
suchen *V* search, seek, look for
Sucht *f* **die** addiction
süchtig addicted
Süden *m* **der** south
südlich south
Südosten *m* **der** southeast
Südwesten *m* **der** southwest
Sünde *f* **die** sin
Super, Superbenzin *n* **das** premium gas
Suppe *f* **die** soup

süß sweet
Süßwasser *n* **das** freshwater
Symbol *n* **das** symbol
Sympathie *f* **die** sympathy
sympathisch sympathetic
Synagoge *f* **die** synagogue
Szene *f* **die** scene

T

Tabak *m* **der** tobacco
Tag *m* **der** day
Tagebuch *n* **das** diary
Tageszeitung *f* **die** daily newspaper
täglich daily
Takt *m* **der** tact, delicacy
Tal *n* **das** valley
Tampon *m* **der** tampon
Tank *m* **der** tank
Tankstelle *f* **die** gas station
tanzen *V* dance
Tarif *m* **der** rate; tariff
Tasche *f* **die** bag; pocket
Taschenbuch *n* **das** paperback
Taschenrechner *m* **der** pocket calculator
Taschentuch *n* **das** handkerchief
Tasse *f* **die** cup
Tastatur *f* **die** keyboard
Taste *f* **die** key
Tat *f* **die** action, act, deed
Tätowierung *f* **die** tattoo
Tatsache *f* **die** fact
taub deaf
Taube *f* **die** pigeon
taubstumm deaf and mute
tauchen *V* dive
taufen *V* baptize

Tausch *m* **der** exchange
tauschen *V* exchange
täuschen *V* deceive, cheat
Taxi *n* **das** taxi
Technik *f* **die** technology; technique
technisch technical
Tee *m* **der** tea
Teil *m/n* **der/das** part
teilen *V* divide, share
Telefonbuch *n* **das** telephone directory
Telefongespräch *n* **das** telephone conversation
Telefonhörer *m* **der** receiver
telefonieren *V2* phone, call
Telegramm *n* **das** telegram
Telephon *n* **das** telephone
Teller *m* **der** plate
Temperament *n* **das** temper, temperament
temperamentvoll vivacious, passionate
Temperatur *f* **die** temperature
Tempo *n* **das** speed, tempo
Tennis *n* **das** tennis
Teppich *m* **der** carpet
Terrasse *f* **die** terrace
Testament *f* **das** testament
testen *V* test, try
teuer expensive
Teufel *m* **der** devil
Text *m* **der** text, words
Theater *n* **das** theater
Theke *f* **die** counter
Thema *n* **das** subject
theoretisch theoretical
Theorie *f* **die** theory
Thermalbad *n* **das** thermal spa
Thermalquelle *f* **die** thermal spring
Thunfisch *m* **der** tuna

tief deep
tiefgefroren deep-frozen
Tiefkühltruhe f **die** freezer
Tier n **das** animal
tierisch animal
Tinte f **die** ink
Tisch m **der** table
Titel m **der** title
Toast m **der** toast
Tochter f **die** daughter
Tod m **der** death
tödlich fatal; lethal
toll great, fantastic; mad, crazy
Ton m **der** sound, tone; clay
Tonne f **die** barrel; (weight) ton
Tor n **das** gate, gateway; goal
Torte f **die** pie
tot dead
total total, complete
töten V kill
Tour f **die** tour, excursion
Tourismus m **der** tourism
Tourist m **der** tourist
Tracht f **die** traditional costume/dress
tragen V* carry
Trambahn f **die** tramway
Träne f **die** tear
Transport m **der** transportation
Trauer f **die** sorrow
Traum m **der** dream
träumen V dream
traurig sad
treffen V* meet; hit; affect
Treffpunkt m **der** meeting point
trennen V separate
Treppe f **die** stairs, staircase

treu faithful
Treue *f* **die** faithfulness, faith, loyalty
Trick *m* **der** trick
trinken *V** drink
Trinkwasser *n* **das** drinking water
trocken dry
trocknen *V* dry
tropfen *V* drop
Tropfen *m* **der** drop
Trost *m* **der** consolation
trösten *V* console, comfort
trotz in spite of, despite
trotzdem nevertheless
Truthahn *m* **der** turkey
Tuch *n* **das** cloth
Tugend *f* **die** virtue
tun do, make
Tür *f* **die** door
Turm *m* **der** tower
Tüte *f* **die** bag, paper bag

U
U-Bahn *f* **die** (Germany) subway
übel bad, evil; sick
Übelkeit *f* **die** sickness
üben *V* exercise, practice
über over; about; above
überall everywhere, all over
Überfall *m* **der** assault
überfallen *V*2* attack, assault
überflüssig unnecessary
Übergewicht *n* **das** overweight
überhaupt generally, actually; **überhaupt kein**
    no ... whatsoever; **überhaupt nicht** not at all
überholen *V2* pass, overtake; overhaul, service
überleben *V2* survive

überlegen *V2* think, reflect
Überlegung *f* **die** consideration, reflection
übermorgen after tomorrow
übernächste second next
übernachten *V2* stay over night
übernehmen *V*2* take over, undertake
überprüfen *V2* check
überraschen *V2* surprise
Überraschung *f* **die** surprise
überreden *V2* persuade
Überschwemmung *f* **die** inundation, flood, deluge
übersetzen *V2* translate
Übersetzung *f* **die** translation
Übersicht *f* **die** survey
übertragbar *V*2* transferable
übertreiben *V** exaggerate
überwachen *V2* supervise, control
überzeugen *V2* convince, persuade
Überzeugung *f* **die** conviction, persuasion
übrig remaining, left over
übrigbleiben *V1* remain
Übung *f* **die** exercise
Ufer *n* **das** shore
Uhr *f* **die** watch, clock
Uhrzeit *f* **die** time
um around; about
umarmen *V2* embrace, hug
Umarmung *f* **die** hug, embrace
umbuchen *V1* transfer, book for another date
umdrehen *V1* turn back, return; turn upside down
Umgebung *f* **die** surroundings, environment
umgekehrt reverse, the other way round
umkehren *V1* turn back, go back
Umlaut *m* **der** vowel mutation (*ä, ö, ü*)
Umriß *m* **der** outline
Umschlag *m* **der** cover; envelope

umschreiben *V*2* transcribe; paraphrase

umsteigen *V1* change

umtauschen *V2* convert, exchange

Umwelt *f* **die** environment

umziehen *V*1* move; **sich umziehen** *V*1* change (clothes)

um zu (in order) to

Umzug *m* **der** procession; move, removal

un- (as prefix) negates the following part of the word

unbegabt untalented

unbekannt unknown

unberechenbar incalculable; dangerous

unbeständig inconstant, unstable

unbewohnt uninhabited

unbezahlbar priceless

unbrennbar nonflammable

und and

undurchsichtig non-transparent

unecht false, not genuine

unehrlich dishonest

unempfindlich insensible

unentgeltlich free, gratis

unerreichbar out of reach

unfähig incapable

Unfall *m* **der** accident

ungebildet uneducated

ungeduldig impatient

ungefähr approximate, about, around

ungefährlich harmless, not dangerous

ungesund unhealthy

Unglück *n* **das** misfortune, bad luck

ungültig invalid

unmöglich impossible

unmoralisch immoral

unregelmäßig irregular

uns us

Unschuld *f* **die** innocence
unschuldig innocent
unser our
unsterblich immortal
unten down; downstairs
unter under, below; **unter uns** between you and me
unterbrechen *V**2 interrupt
Unterbrechung *f* **die** interruption
unterdrücken *V2* suppress; oppress
Unterdrückung *f* **die** suppression
Unterführung *f* **die** underpass
Untergang *m* **der** ruin, fall
unterhalten *V**2 maintain; entertain, amuse
Unterhaltung *f* **die** conversation; entertainment,
    amusement
Unterhemd *m* **das** undershirt
Unterhose *f* **die** underpants
unternehmen *V**2 undertake, attempt
Unternehmen *n* **das** enterprise, company
Unterricht *m* **der** instruction, lessons
unterrichten *V2* teach, instruct
Unterschied *m* **der** difference, distinction
untersuchen *V2* inquire, examine; analyze;
    explore; investigate
Untersuchung *f* **die** inquiry; investigation; analysis
unterwegs on the way, in transit
unverbindlich informal; without obligation
unvergänglich everlasting
unverheiratet unmarried, single
unverschämt impudent, impertinent
unverständlich unintelligible
Unwetter *n* **das** thunderstorm
unwichtig insignificant
unzufrieden discontented
Urin *m* **der** urine
Urkunde *f* **die** document, record

Urlaub *m* **der** holiday, vacation
Urlauber *m* **der** vacationist
Urteil *n* **das** judgement; opinion

V

Vase *f* **die** vase
Vater *m* **der** father
Vegetarier *m* **der** vegetarian
Ventil *n* **das** valve
verabreden *V2* appoint; agree (upon)
Verabredung *f* **die** appointment
verachten *V2* despise
verändern *V2* change, alter
Veränderung *f* **die** alteration, change
verantwortlich responsible
Verantwortung *f* **die** responsibility
Verb *n* **das** verb
Verband *m* **der** bandage; federation, union
verbessern *V2* improve
verbieten *V** forbid, prohibit
verbinden *V*2* bandage; connect; unite, combine
Verbindung *f* **die** connection; union, combination
Verbot *n* **das** prohibition, ban
verboten forbidden
Verbrauch *m* **der** consumption
verbrauchen *V2* consume, use up
Verbrechen *n* **das** crime
verbrennen *V*2* burn
Verdacht *m* **der** suspicion
verdächtig suspect
verderben *V*2* rot; perish
verdienen *V2* gain; deserve
vereinfachen *V2* simplify
vereinigt united
Verfassung *f* **die** constitution; disposition
verfolgen *V2* pursue

Vergangenheit *f* **die** past
vergeben *V**2 forgive; give away
vergessen *V**2 forget
Vergleich *m* **der** comparison
vergleichen *V**2 compare
vergrößern *V*2 enlarge, magnify
Verhalten *n* **das** behavior
verhalten (sich) *V**2 behave
Verhältnis *n* **das** relation, relationship
verheiratet married
verkaufen *V*2 sell
Verkäufer *m* **der** salesclerk
Verkäuferin *f* **die** salesclerk
Verkehr *m* **der** traffic; transportation
verkehren *V*2 operate (bus or metro)
verkehrt wrong, false
verkleinern *V*2 reduce in size, make smaller
Verlag *m* **der** publisher
verlangen *V*2 demand, claim; desire
Verlangen *n* **das** desire; demand
verlieben (sich) *V*2 fall in love
verliebt in love
verlieren *V**2 lose
verlobt engaged
Verlobte *m* **der** fiancé
Verlobte *f* **die** fiancée
Verlobung *f* **die** engagement
verloren lost
vermieten *V*2 rent, let
vermuten *V*2 suppose, presume
Vernunft *f* **die** reason
vernünftig rational, reasonable
verpassen *V*2 miss
verreisen *V*2 travel, go on a trip
verrückt mad, crazy
verschieden different, distinct

verschließen *V*2* lock
Verschluß *m* **der** lock; fastener
Versehen *n* **das** mistake; **aus Versehen** by mistake
versichert insured
Versicherung *f* **die** insurance; affirmation
verspäten (sich) *V2* be late
Verspätung *f* **die** delay
Verstand *m* **der** intellect, brains, reason
verstehen *V*2* understand
Versuch *m* **der** attempt, trial; experiment
versuchen *V2* try, attempt; taste
verteidigen *V2* defend
Verteidigung *f* **die** defense
Vertrag *m* **der** contract
vertrauen *V2* trust
Vertrauen *n* **das** confidence, trust
verwandt related
Verwandte *m* **der** male relative
Verwandte *f* **die** female relative
verwechseln *V2* confound, mix up; change by
    mistake
verwunden *V2* wound
verzeihen *V*2* forgive, pardon
Verzeihung! Excuse me! Pardon!
Vieh *n* **das** cattle
viel much
viele many
Vielen Dank! Thank you!
vielleicht maybe, perhaps
Viertel *n* **das** fourth part; (wine) ¼ liter
Villa *f* **die** villa
Virus *m/n* **der/das** virus
Visum *n* **das** visa
Vogel *m* **der** bird
Volk *n* **das** people
voll full; complete, entire; drunk

volljährig adult

Vollkornbrot *n* **das** whole-meal bread

Vollmacht *f* **die** proxy, authority

von from; of; about; **von vorn** from the beginning; from the front

vor in front of; before; ago

voraus ahead; **im voraus** in advance

vorbei past; along

vorgestern the day before yesterday

Vorhang *m* **der** curtain

Vormittag *m* **der** morning

vorn, vorne in front, before, ahead; **von vorn** from the front, from the beginning

Vorname *m* **der** name

Vorort *m* **der** suburb

Vorrat *m* **der** stock, supply

Vorschrift *f* **die** prescription

Vorsicht *f* **die** caution, care; **Vorsicht!** Caution! Beware! Watch out!

vorsichtig careful, cautious

Vorteil *m* **der** advantage

W

wach awake

Wachs *n* **das** wax

wachsen *V** * grow

Wachstum *n* **das** growth

Waffe *f* **die** weapon, arm

wagen *V* dare

Wagen *m* **der** car, vehicle

Wahl *f* **die** choice

wählen *V* choose, elect

wahnsinnig crazy

wahr true

während during

Wahrheit *f* **die** truth

wahrscheinlich probably

Währung *f* **die** currency

Wald *m* **der** forest

Walzer *m* **der** waltz

Wand *f* **die** wall

wandern *V* wander, hike

Wanderung *f* **die** hike

wann when; **seit wann** how long, since when

Ware *f* **die** merchandise, ware

Warenhaus *n* **das** shopping center, shopping mall

warm warm

Wärme *f* **die** warmth

warnen *V* warn

Warnung *f* **die** warning

warten *V* wait

warum why

was what

Wäsche *f* **die** laundry

waschen *V** wash

Wasser *n* **das** water

Wasserleitung *f* **die** water pipes

wechseln *V* change; **Geld wechseln** change money

wecken *V* wake up

weder ... noch ... neither ... nor ...

weg away; **weit weg** far away

Weg *m* **der** way

wegen because of

wegfahren *V*1* go away, leave

wegwerfen *V*1* throw away

weh tun hurt oneself

weich soft

Weihnachten *n* **das** Christmas

weil because

Wein *m* **der** wine

Weinberg *m* **der** vineyard

weinen *V* cry

Weinkeller *m* **der** wine cellar
weiß white
Weißbier *n* **das** wheat beer
Weißbrot *n* **das** white bread
weit far; **weit weg** far away
weiter farther, further
weitergehen *V*1* walk on
Weizen *m* **der** wheat
welche what, which, who
Welle *f* **die** wave
Welt *f* **die** world
Weltall, Weltraum *m* **der** space, universe
wem to whom
wen whom
wenig few, little
wenn if
wer who
Werbung *f* **die** publicity
werden *V** become, be
Werk *n* **das** work
wert worth
Wert *m* **der** value; worth
Wesen *n* **das** creature, being
wessen whose
Westen *m* **der** west
westlich west
Wette *f* **die** bet
wetten *V* bet
Wetter *n* **das** weather
wichtig important
widerlich disgusting, obnoxious
wie how
Wie bitte? (I beg your) pardon?
wieder again
wiedergeben *V*1* give back, return; reproduce
wiederholen *V2* repeat

Wiederholung *f* **die** repetition
wiedersehen *V*1* see again, meet again
Wiedervereinigung *f* **die** reunification
Wiese *f* **die** meadow
wild wild
Wild *n* **das** game
Wille *m* **der** will
willkommen welcome
Wind *m* **der** wind
Windel *f* **die** diaper
Winkel *m* **der** angle
winken *V** wave, make a sign
Winter *m* **der** winter
Winzer *m* **der** wine grower
wirken *V* work, function
wirklich real, really
Wirt *m* **der** host, landlord
Wirtin *f* **die** host, landlord
Wirtschaft *f* **die** economy; restaurant, saloon
wissen *V** know
Witz *m* **der** joke; wit
wo who
Woche *f* **die** weak
woher from where
wohin where (in which direction)
Wohl *n* **das** welfare, prosperity; **Zum Wohl!** To
    your health!
wohnen *V* live
Wohngebiet *n* **das** residential area
Wohnung *f* **die** apartment
Wolke *f* **die** cloud
wollen *V* wish, want
woraus out of what, from what
worin in what; in which
Wort *n* **das** word

Wörterbuch *n* **das** dictionary
worüber about what
wund sore, wounded
Wunder *n* **das** miracle, wonder
wunderbar wonderful
wunderschön very beautiful, wonderful
Wunsch *m* **der** wish, desire
wünschen *V* wish
Würde *f* **die** dignity
Würfel *m* **der** dice; cube
Wurm *m* **der** worm
Wurst *f* **die** sausage
Wurzel *f* **die** root
Wut *f* **die** rage, fury

Z

Zahl *f* **die** number
zahlen *V* pay
zählen *V* count
Zahn *m* **der** tooth
zart tender
zärtlich tenderly
Zaun *m* **der** fence
Zeh *f* **der** toe
zehnmal ten times
zeichnen *V* draw
zeigen *V* show, indicate, demonstrate
Zeit *f* **die** time
Zeitung *f* **die** newspaper
Zelle *f* **die** cell
Zelt *n* **das** tent
Zentimeter *m* **der** centimeter
Zentrum *n* **das** center, middle
Zettel *m* **der** slip, piece of paper
Zeug *n* **das** stuff

ziehen V^* pull; draw a line
Ziel *n* **das** target, aim
zielen *V* aim
ziemlich quite
Zigarette *f* **die** cigarette
Zigarre *f* **die** cigar
Zigeuner *m* **der** Gypsy
Zimmer *n* **das** room
zirka about, approximately
Zitrone *f* **die** lemon
zittern *V* tremble, shake, shiver
Zoll *m* **der** customs
zollfrei duty-free
zollpflichtig dutiable
Zoo *m* **der** zoo
zu to, towards; too; closed
Zucker *m* **der** sugar
zuerst first, at first
Zufall *m* **der** chance, coincidence
zufällig accidental, by chance
Zug *m* **der** train
zu Hause at home
Zukunft *f* **die** future
zum = zu dem; Zum Wohl! To your health!
zumachen *V1* close, shut
Zunge *f* **die** tongue
zurück back, backwards
zurückgehen V^*1 return, go back
zurückkommen V^*1 come again, come back
zusammen together
zusammenarbeiten *V1* work together
zusammenwachsen *V1* grow together
zuschauen *V1* watch
zusehen V^*1 watch
zuständig competent

zuverlässig reliable
zuviel too much
zuwenig too little
Zweck *m* **der** purpose, object
Zwiebel *f* **die** onion
Zweifel *m* **der** doubt
Zweig *m* **der** branch
zweimal twice
zweit zu zweit by twos
Zwilling *m* **der** twin
zwingen *V** compel, force
zwischen between
Zwischenlandung *f* **die** stop-over

ENGLISH-GERMAN DICTIONARY

A

a *art.* ein
able fähig
about etwa, circa, ungefähr, von, über; um; **about what** worüber
above oben
accident Unfall *m* der
accidental zufällig
accompany begleiten *V2*, mitgehen *V*1*
according to nach
achieve schaffen *V**, erreichen *V2*
acid Säure *f* die; sauer
across hinüber
act Tat *f* die, Akt *m* der; handeln *V*
action Tat *f* die, Handlung *f* die
actually eigentlich, überhaupt
addicted süchtig
addiction Sucht *f* die
address Adresse *f* die
adjective Adjektiv *n* das
adjust stellen *V*
admittance Eintritt *m* der
adult volljährig, erwachsen
advantage Vorteil *n* der
adverb Adverb *n* das
advice Rat *m* der
advise raten *V**
advocate Anwalt *m* der, Rechtsanwalt *m* der
affair Geschäft *n* das; Angelegenheit *f* die, Sache *f* die
affect betreffen *V*2*, treffen *V**
affirmation Versicherung *f* die

after nach, nachher

after this danach

after tomorrow übermorgen

afternoon Nachmittag *m* der

afterwards nachher, danach

again wieder

against gegen

against each other gegeneinander

against that dagegen

agency Amt *n* das, Agentur *f* die

ago vor

agree übereinstimmen *V1*, verabreden *V2*

ahead vorn, vorne, voraus

aim zielen *V*; Ziel *n* das

air Luft *f* die

alike gleich

all alle, ganz

all over überall

allow gestatten *V2*, erlauben *V2*; lassen *V*

almost fast

alone allein

along vorbei

Alps Alpen *f/pl.* die

already schon

also auch

alter verändern *V2*

alteration Veränderung *f* die

always immer

ambulance Krankenwagen *m* der

amount Menge *f* die

amuse unterhalten *V*2*

amusement Unterhaltung *f* die

analysis Analyse *f* die, Untersuchung *f* die

analyze analysieren *V2*, untersuchen *V2*

and und

angel Engel *m* der
anger Ärger *m* der; ärgern *V*
angle Winkel *m* der
angry wütend, ärgerlich
animal Tier *n* das; tierisch
announce anmelden *V1*, melden *V*
announcement Durchsage *f* die, Meldung *f* die
annoyance Ärger *m* der
answer Antwort *f* die; antworten *V*
ant Ameise *f* die
antenna Antenne *f* die
antidote Gegenmittel *n* das
anxiety Angst *f* die
any irgend, irgendein
anyone jeder
anytime jederzeit
anywhere überall
apartment Wohnung *f* die
apologize entschuldigen *V2*; Entschuldigung *f* die
apparatus Apparat *m* der
appear scheinen *V**
appetite Appetit *m* der
apple Apfel *m* der
application Anmeldung *f* die
apply for *V1* anmelden
appoint verabreden *V2*
appointment Verabredung *f* die
approximate ungefähr
approximately etwa, circa
April April *m* der
area Gegend *f* die
argue streiten *V**
arm Arm *m* der; Waffe *f* die
army Militär *n* das
around ungefähr, um

arrange einrichten *V1*, arrangieren *V2*, ordnen *V*
arrangement Arrangement *n* das, Ordnung *f* die
arrival Ankunft *f* die
arrive ankommen *V*1*, kommen *V**
arrow Pfeil *m* der
art Kunst *f* die
artificial künstlich
artist Künstler *m* der, Maler *m* der
as als; da; **as if** als ob
as far as soweit, bis
ask fragen *V*; bitten *V**; fordern *V*
ass Arsch *m* der (*vulgar*)
assault Überfall *m* der; überfallen *V*2*
at an, bei
at first zuerst
at home daheim, zu hause, Zuhause *n* das
at least mindestens
at night nachts
at once sofort, auf einmal
at present nun
at that time damals
at the same time gleichzeitig
athletic sportlich
atmosphere Stimmung *f* die
attack angreifen *V*1*, überfallen *V*2*; Angriff *m* der
attempt Versuch *m* der; versuchen *V2*,
   unternehmen *V*2*
audience Publikum *n* das
August August *m* der
author Autor *m* der, Schriftsteller *m* der
authority Behörde *f* die
autobus Autobus *m* der, Bus *m* der
average Durchschnitt *m* der; durchschnittlich
await erwarten *V2*
awake wach; aufwachen *V1*
away fort; weg; **far away** weit weg

B

baby Baby *n* das
back rückwärts; zurück
backpack Rucksack *m* der
backwards rückwärts; zurück
bacon Speck *m* der
bacteria Bakterien *n/pl.* die
bad schlecht; schlimm; übel; böse
bad luck Pech *n* das
bag Tasche *f* die, Tüte *f* die
bake backen *V**
baker Bäcker *m* der
bakery Bäckerei *f* die
balance Gleichgewicht *n* das; Waage *f* die
balcony Balkon *m* der; (of a theater) Loge *f* die
ball Ball *m* der, Kugel *f* die
ban Verbot *n* das
band Band *n* das; (music) Band *f* die
bandage verbinden *V*2;* Verband *m* der,
    Bandage *f* die
bang Knall *m* der
bank Bank *f* die
banknote Geldschein *m* der
banner Fahne *f* die
baptize taufen *V*
bar Bar *f* die, Café *n* das, Kneipe *f* die
barbecue grillen *V*
barrel Faß *n* das, Tonne *f* die
barrier Sperre *f* die
basket Korb *m* der
bath Bad *n* das
bathe baden *V*
bathroom Bad *n* das; Toilette *f* die
battle Kampf *m* der
be sein *V*, werden *V**; liegen *V**
be able können *V*

be absent fehlen *V*
be allowed dürfen *V**
be ashamed sich schämen *V*
be born geboren werden *V**
be called heißen *V**
be drunk betrunken sein *V**
be enough genügen *V2*
be happy sich freuen *V*
be interested in sich interessieren *V2*
be late sich verspäten *V2*
be missing fehlen *V*
be named heißen *V**
be of use nützen *V*, nützlich sein *V*, nutzen *V*
be permitted dürfen *V**
be silent schweigen *V**
be sorry bedauern *V2*; sich entschuldigen *V2*, leid
   tun *V*2*
be useful nutzen *V*, nützen *V*, nützlich sein *V*
be valid gelten *V**
beach Strand *m* der
bean Bohne *f* die
beard Bart *m* der
beat schlagen *V**
beautiful schön; **very beautiful** wunderschön
beauty Schönheit *f* die
because weil, da, denn
because of wegen
become werden *V**
bed Bett *n* das
bedroom Schlafzimmer *n* das
beef Rindfleisch *n* das
beer Bier *n* das
beer garden Biergarten *m* der
before bevor, vor
before yesterday vorgestern
beg betteln *V*

beggar Bettler *m* der
begin anfangen *V1*
beginning Beginn *m* der, Anfang *m* der
behave sich benehmen *V*2*, sich verhalten *V*2*
behavior Verhalten *n* das, Benehmen *n* das
behind hinten, hinter; **behind it** dahinter
being Wesen *n* das; Sein *n* das
believe glauben *V*
belly Bauch *m* der
belong gehören *V*
below unter
belt Gürtel *m* der
benefit Nutzen *m* der
berry Beere *f* die
beside neben
besides neben, nebenbei; außer
best Beste *m* der, Beste *f* die; am besten
bet Wette *f* die; wetten *V*
better besser
between zwischen
between you and me unter uns
beverage Getränk *n* das
bible Bibel *f* die
bicycle Fahrrad *n* das
big dick, fett
bike Fahrrad *n* das
bill Rechnung *f* die; Geldschein *m* der
bird Vogel *m* der
birth Geburt *f* die
birthday Geburtstag *m* der
birthplace Geburtsort *m* der
bit bißchen, ein
bite beißen *V**
bitter bitter
black schwarz
bladder Blase *f* die

blanket Decke *f* die
bless segnen *V*
blessing Segen *m* der
blind blind
blockade Sperre *f* die
blond blond
blood Blut *n* das
blue blau
boardinghouse Pension *f* die
boat Boot *n* das, Schiff *n* das
body Körper *m* der
bonbon Bonbon *n* das
bone Knochen *m* der
book Buch *n* das; buchen *V,* bestellen *V2,*
    reservieren *V2*
book for another date umbuchen *V1*
boot Stiefel *m* der
border Grenze *f* die
border crossing Grenzübergang *m* der
boring langweilig
born geboren
borrow leihen *V*
both beide, beides
bottle Flasche *f* die
bouquet Strauß *m* der
boutique Boutique *f* die
bowels Eingeweide *n/pl.* die
bowl Schüssel *f* die, Schale *f* die
boy Junge *m* der
boyfriend Freund *m* der
brain Gehirn *n* das, Kopf *m* der
brains (smarts) Verstand *m* der
branch Zweig *m* der; Filiale *f* die
brave mutig
bread Brot *n* das

break Pause *f* die; Bremse *f* die; brechen *V**, zerbrechen *V*2*

breakfast Frühstück *n* das

break in einbrechen *V*1*

breast Brust *f* die

breath Atem *m* der; atmen *V*

bribe bestechen *V*2*

bride Braut *f* die

bridge Brücke *f* die

brief kurz

bright hell

brilliant genial

bring bringen *V**

bring along mitbringen *V*1*

broad breit

broadcast senden *V*

broken kaputt

brother Bruder *m* der

brother-in-law Schwager *m* der

brown braun

brush Bürste *f* die

brutal brutal

bucket Eimer *m* der

budget Budget *n* das

buffet Buffet *n* das

bug Käfer *m* der

build bauen *V*

bullet Kugel *f* die, Geschoß *n* das

bunch Bündel *n* das, Strauß *m* der

bunch of flowers Blumenstraß *m* der

burglar Einbrecher *m* der

burglarize einbrechen *V*1*

burn brennen *V**, verbrennen *V*2*

bus Bus *m* der, Omnibus *m* der, Autobus *m* der

bush Busch *m* der

business Geschäft *n* das, Business *n* das; geschäftlich

business district Geschäftsviertel *n* das
businessman Geschäftsmann *m* der;
    Kaufmann *m* der
business trip Geschäftsreise *f* die
busy (telephone) belegt
but aber, sondern; doch
butcher Metzger *m* der
butter Butter *f* die
button Knopf *m* der
buy kaufen *V,* einkaufen *V1*
by bei, von; durch
by chance zufällig
by himself/herself von allein
by means of mit, mit Hilfe
by night nachts

C

cabbage Kohl *m* der
cabin Kabine *f* die
cable Kabel *n* das, Seil *n* das; **cable car/railway**
    Seilbahn *f* die, Bergbahn *f* die
café Café *n* das
cake Kuchen *m* der
calculate rechnen *V*
calculation Rechnung *f* die
calf Kalb *n* das
call rufen *V**, nennen *V**; anrufen *V1*, telefonieren
    V2; Anruf *m* der
calm still, ruhig; beruhigen *V2*
calm down beruhigen *V2*
camera Kamera *f* die
camp Lager *n* das
can Dose *f* die
candle Kerze *f* die
can opener Dosenöffner *m* der
car Auto *n* das, Wagen *m* der

car rental Autovermietung *f* die
card Karte *f* die
care Vorsicht *f* die, Fürsorge *f* die, Sorge *f* die; sorgen (für) *V*
careful vorsichtig, sorgfältig
caress streicheln *V*
carpet Teppich *m* der
carry tragen *V**
case Fall *m* der
cash bar, in bar; Bargeld *n* das
cashier Kasse *f* die
cash register Kasse *f* die
casino Spielkasino *n* das
cask Faß *n* das
cassette Kassette *f* die
castle Schloß *n* das, Burg *f* die
cat Katze *f* die; (tomcat) Kater *m* der
cattle Vieh *n* das
caution Vorsicht *f* die; **Caution!** Vorsicht!, Achtung!
cautious vorsichtig
cave Höhle *f* die
celebration Feier *f* die
cell Zelle *f* die
Celsius Celsius *m* der
center Zentrum *n* das, Mitte *f* die
center of gravity Schwerpunkt *m* der
centimeter Zentimeter *m* der
chain Kette *f* die
chair Stuhl *m* der
chance Chance *f* die, Zufall *m* der
chancellor Kanzler *m* der
change Veränderung *f* die, Wechsel *m* der; ändern *V*, umsteigen *V1*, wechseln *V*, verändern *V2*; (clothes) sich umziehen *V*1*
change by mistake verwechseln *V2*
change money Geld wechseln *V*

channel Kanal *m* der

character Charakter *m* der

charcoal Holzkohle *f* die, Kohle *f* die

cheap billig

cheat betrügen *V*2*, täuschen *V*; Betrug *m* der

check Scheck *m* der; Kontrolle *f* die,
Überprüfung *f* die; überprüfen *V2*,
kontrollieren *V2*, nachsehen *V*1*

cheers! prost!

cheese Käse *m* der

chicken Huhn *n* das

chief Haupt-, Haupt *n* das, Spitze *f* die; Leiter *m* der,
Chef *m* der

child Kind *n* das

choice Wahl *f* die

choir Chor *m* der

choose wählen *V*, aussuchen *V1*

Christmas Weihnachten *n* das

church Kirche *f* die

church tower Kirchturm *m* der

cigar Zigarre *f* die

cigarette Zigarette *f* die

cinema Kino *n* das

circa circa

circle Kreis *m* der

citadel Burg *f* die

citizen Bürger *m* der

city Stadt *f* die, Ort *m* der

claim verlangen *V2*

class Klasse *f* die

classic klassisch

clause Satz *m* der

clay Ton *m* der

clean putzen *V*, reinigen *V*; sauber, rein, ordentlich

clear klar

clever klug, intelligent, schlau

cliché Klischee *n* das
client Kunde *m* der
climate Klima *n* das
clock Uhr *f* die
cloister Kloster *n* das
close schließen *V**, zumachen *V1*, schließen *V**, zumachen *V1*; nahe; **close by** in der Nähe; **close to** nahe bei
closed geschlossen, zu
closet Schrank *m* der
cloth Tuch *n* das
clothes Kleidung *f* die
clothing Kleidung *f* die
cloud Wolke *f* die
coal Kohle *f* die
coat Mantel *m* der
cockroach Kakerlake *f* die, Küchenschabe *f* die
coffee Kaffee *m* der
coin Münze *f* die, Geldstück *n* das
coincidence Zufall *m* der
cold kalt, kühl
colleague Kollege *m* der
color Farbe *f* die
comb Kamm *m* der
combination Kombination *f* die, Verbindung *f* die
combine verbinden *V*2*, kombinieren *V2*
come kommen *V**; **Come in!** Herein!
come again wiederkommen *V*1*, zurückkommen *V*1*
come back zurückkommen *V*1*, wiederkommen *V*1*
comfort trösten *V*
comfortable bequem, komfortabel, gemütlich
comic komisch
commerce Handel *m* der

commercial gewerblich, kaufmännisch;
 Werbespot *m* der
commercial treaty Handelsvertrag *m* der
commission Auftrag *m* der
common gewöhnlich, gemeinsam, alltäglich,
 allgemein
communicate mitteilen *V1*; kommunizieren *V2*
community Gemeinschaft *f* die, Gemeinde *f* die
company Gesellschaft *f* die, Begleitung *f* die,
 Gemeinschaft *f* die; Unternehmen *f* das,
 Gesellschaft *f* die, Firma *f* die
compare vergleichen *V*2*
comparison Vergleich *m* der
compel zwingen *V**
competent fähig; zuständig
competition Konkurrenz *f* die
complain sich beklagen *V2*, sich beschweren *V2*,
 klagen *V*
complaint Beschwerde *f* die, Klage *f* die
complete voll, komplett, total
compliment Kompliment *n* das
composer Komponist *m* der
conceited eingebildet
conclusion Abschluß *m* der
condiment Gewürz *n* das
conference Konferenz *f* die, Sitzung *f* die
confidence Vertrauen *n* das
confound verwechseln *V2*
congestion Stau *m* der, Verstopfung *f* die
congregation Gemeinde *f* die
connect verbinden *V*2*
connection Verbindung *f* die
conscious bewußt
consider beachten *V2*
consideration Überlegung *f* die
consolation Trost *m* der

console trösten *V*

constitution Verfassung *f* die

consult um Rat fragen *V*

consulting room (doctor's office) Praxis *f* die

consume verbrauchen *V2*, konsumieren *V2*

consumption Verbrauch *m* der

contact (person) Kontakt *m* der; kontaktieren *V2*, in Kontakt treten *V**

content Gehalt *m* der, Inhalt *m* der

continuation Fortsetzung *f* die

continue fortfahren *V*1*

contraception Empfängnisverhütung *f* die

contract Vertrag *m* der

contrary Gegenteil *n* das

control kontrollieren *V2*, überwachen *V2*; Macht *f* die, Kontrolle *f* die

convenient bequem, vorteilhaft

conversation Gespräch *n* das, Konversation *f* die, Unterhaltung *f* die

convert umtauschen *V2*, konvertieren *V2*

conviction Überzeugung *f* die

convince überzeugen *V2*

cook Koch *m* der; kochen *V*

cookie Keks *m* der, Plätzchen *n* das

cool kühl; lässig

copy kopieren *V2*; Kopie *f* die

corner Ecke *f* die

corpse Leiche *f* die

correct korrekt, richtig

cost kosten *V*

cotton Baumwolle *f* die

cough husten *V;* Husten *m* der

count zählen *V*

count on rechnen *V* mit

counter Theke *f* die, Buffet *n* das; Schalter *m* der

counterfeit money Falschgeld *n* das

country Land *n* das

countryside Land *n* das

couple Paar *n* das, Pärchen *n* das

couple of ein paar

courage Mut *m* der

courageous mutig

course Gang *m* der, Gericht *n* das; Kurs *m* der

court Gericht *n* das; Hof *m* der

courtyard Hof *m* der

cover Decke *f* die; Umschlag *m* der; bedecken *V2*

coverage Reportage *f* die

cow Kuh *f* die, Rind *n* das

cozy gemütlich

cracker Keks *m* der, Plätzchen *n* das

cramp Krampf *m* der

crane fly Schnake *f* die

crash Sturz *m* der

crazy wahnsinnig, verrückt, toll

create schaffen *V*2*, erschaffen *V*2*

creature Wesen *n* das

crime Verbrechen *n* das

cripple Krüppel *m* der

criticism Kritik *f* die

criticize kritisieren *V2*

cross Kreuz *n* das; quer

crossing Kreuzung *f* die

crossroads Kreuzung *f* die

crown Krone *f* die

cry weinen *V,* schreien *V**; Schrei *m* der

cube Würfel *m* der

cuisine Küche *f* die

cultural kulturell

culture Kultur *f* die

cumin Kümmel *m* der

cup Tasse *f* die, Schale *f* die

curds Quark *m* der

cure Kur *f* die; heilen *V*
currency Währung *f* die
current Strom *m* der; Strömung *f* die
curse fluchen *V;* Fluch *m* der
curtain Vorhang *m* der
custom Sitte *f* die, Brauch *m* der,
  Gewohnheit *f* die
customs Zoll *m* der

D

daily täglich, alltäglich
daily newspaper Tageszeitung *f* die
dance tanzen *V*
dandruff Schuppen *f/pl.* die
danger Gefahr *f* die; (to one's life) Lebensgefahr *f* die
dangerous gefährlich; (to one's life) lebensgefährlich
dare wagen *V*
dark dunkel
darkness Dunkelheit *f* die
date Datum *n* das
daughter Tochter *f* die
day Tag *m* der
day-care center Kindertagesstätte *f* die
dead tot
deaf taub; **deaf and mute** taubstumm
dealer Kaufmann *m* der, Händler *m* der
dear nett, lieb
death Tod *m* der
debt Schuld *f* die, Schulden *f/pl.* die
deceive täuschen *V*
December Dezember *m* der
decide entscheiden *V*2*
decided beschlossen, entschieden
decision Entscheidung *f* die
deed Tat *f* die
deep tief

deep-frozen tiefgefroren

defect Fehler *m* der

defend verteidigen *V2*

defense Verteidigung *f* die

degree Grad *m* der; Stufe *f* die; **degree
   centigrade** Grad Celsius *n* das

delay Verspätung *f* die; sich verspäten *V2*

deliberate bewußt, absichtlich

delicacy Takt *m* der

delicate delikat, fein

delicious delikat, lecker

delight Lust *f* die, Genuß *m* der, Freude *f* die

deluge Überschwemmung *f* die

demand fordern *V,* verlangen *V2;* Verlangen *n* das

demonstrate zeigen *V*

deodorant Deodorant *n* das

departure Abreise *f* die, Abfahrt *f* die, (of a plane)
   Abflug *m* der

deposit Lager *n* das

describe beschreiben *V*2*

deserve verdienen *V2*

desire verlangen *V2*, wünschen *V;* Verlangen *n* das,
   Lust *f* die, Wunsch *m* der

despise verachten *V2*

despite trotz

determined entschlossen, entschieden

device Gerät *n* das

devil Teufel *m* der

diabetic Diabetiker *m* der

dialect Dialekt *m* der

diaper Windel *f* die

diarrhea Durchfall *m* der

diary Tagebuch *n* das

dice Würfel *m* der

dictionary Wörterbuch *n* das, Lexikon *n* das

die sterben *V**

diesel Diesel *n* das
diet Diät *f* die
difference Unterschied *m* der
different anders, verschieden
difficult schwierig, schwer
dignity Würde *f* die
diligent fleißig
dinner Abendessen *n* das
diplomat Diplomat *m* der
diplomatic diplomatisch
direct direkt
direct dialing Durchwahl *f* die
direction Richtung *f* die; Direktion *f* die, Leitung *f* die
directions, directions for use Gebrauchsanweisung *f* die
director Direktor *m* der
dirt Schmutz *m* der, Dreck *m* der
dirty schmutzig
disappoint enttäuschen *V2*
disappointment Enttäuschung *f* die
discontented unzufrieden
discuss diskutieren
discussion Diskussion *f* die
disease Krankheit *f* die
disgust Ekel *m* der
disgusting eklig, widerlich
dish Gericht *n* das, Speise *f* die
dishonest unehrlich
disk Diskette *f* die, Scheibe *f* die
dismiss entlassen *V*2*
disposition Verfassung *f* die, Disposition *f* die
dispute Streit *m* der
distance Strecke *f* die
distinct verschieden
distinction Unterschied *m* der

district Bezirk *m* der
disturb stören *V*
disturbance Störung *f* die
dive tauchen *V*
divide teilen *V*
divorce Scheidung *f* die
divorced geschieden
dizzy schwindelig
do tun *V**, machen *V*
doctor Arzt *m* der, Doktor *m* der
document Urkunde *f* die
dog Hund *m* der
donation Stiftung *f* die
done fertig; (cooked food) gar
door Tür *f* die
door-plate Schild *n* das
double doppelt
doubt Zweifel *m* der
down unten, herunter, hinunter
downstairs unten, hinunter, herunter
downtown Stadtzentrum *f* das, Geschäftsviertel *n* das; im Stadtzentrum
drama Drama *n* das
draw zeichnen *V,* malen *V*; ziehen *V**
dream Traum *m* der; träumen *V*
dress (apparel) Kleid *n* das, Anzug *m* der; kleiden *V*, anziehen *V*1*
drink trinken *V**; Getränk *n* das
drinking water Trinkwasser *n* das
drip Fallenlassen *V*1*
drive fahren *V**
driver Fahrer *m* der
drop Tropfen *m* der; tropfen *V*
drug Medikament *n* das, Droge *f* die
drugstore Drogerie *f* die
drunk betrunken

drunkenness Rausch *m* der
dry trocken; trocknen *V*
dumb dumm
duplicate Kopie *f* die
duration Dauer *f* die
during während
dutiable zollpflichtig
duty Pflicht *f* die
duty-free zollfrei

E

ear Ohr *n* das
early früh
earth Erde *f* die
east Osten *m* der; östlich
easy leicht
eat essen *V**
ebb tide Ebbe *f* die
economy Wirtschaft *f* die, Ökonomie *f* die
edge Rand *m* der
edition Ausgabe *f* die, Edition *f* die
educate erziehen *V*2*
education Erziehung *f* die
egg Ei *n* das
egg white Eiweiß *n* das
elect wählen *V*
electric elektrisch
electrical elektrisch
electricity Elektrizität *f* die, Strom *m* der
electronic elektronisch
else sonst
emancipation Emanzipation *f* die
embarrassing peinlich
embrace umarmen *V*2; Umarmung *f* die
emergency Notfall *m* der
emergency doctor Notarzt *m* der

employment Stellung *f* die
empty leer
encyclopedia Lexikon *n* das
end Ende *n* das; ausgehen *V*1*, enden *V*
ending Endung *f* die
enemy Feind *m* der, Feindin *f* die
energy Energie *f* die
engaged verlobt
engagement Verlobung *f* die
English englisch
enlarge vergrößern *V2*
enough genug
enroll for anmelden
enterprise Unternehmen *n* das
entertain unterhalten *V*2*
entertainment Unterhaltung *f* die
entire ganz, voll, gesamt
entrance Eingang *m* der
entry Eintritt *m* der, Einreise *f* die
envelope Briefumschlag *m* der, Umschlag *m* der
environment Umwelt *f* die, Umgebung *f* die
envy Neid *m* der
equal gleich
equilibrium Gleichgewicht *n* das
equipment Ausrüstung *f* die; Einrichtung *f* die
escape Flucht *f* die, Rettung *f* die
especially besonders, extra, (prefix) extra-
establishment Einrichtung *f* die
eternal ewig
Eurocheque (European money order) Euroscheck
   m der
Europe Europa
European Europäer *m* der, Europäerin *f* die;
   europäisch
even sogar, glatt, gerade
evening Abend *m* der

everlasting unvergänglich

every alle; jede *f*, jeder *m*, jedes *n*

everybody jede *f*, jeder *m*, jedes *n*

everyone jede *f*, jeder *m*, jedes *n*

everything alles

everywhere überall

evidence Beweis *m* der

evil schlecht, böse, schlimm, übel

exact genau, exakt

exaggerate übertreiben *V**

examination Überprüfung *f* die, Prüfung *f* die;
   Examen *n* das

examine untersuchen *V2*

example Beispiel *n* das

except außer

except that außer daß

exception Ausnahme *f* die

exchange tauschen *V,* umtauschen *V2;* Tausch *m* der

exciting aufregend, spannend

exclusive exklusiv

excursion Ausflug *m* der, Ausfahrt *f* die, Tour *f* die

excuse entschuldigen *V2;* Entschuldigung *f* die

excuse me! Verzeihung!

exercise Übung *f* die; üben *V,* trainieren *V2*

exit Ausgang *m* der; (highway) Ausfahrt *f* die

expect erwarten *V2*

expense Ausgabe *f* die

expensive teuer

experiment Versuch *m* der, Experiment *n* das

explain erklären

explanation Erklärung *f* die

explore untersuchen *V2*

export Ausfuhr *f* die; Export *m* der

express per Expreß, Expreß *m* der; ausdrücken
   V1, äußern *V*

extension number Durchwahl *f* die

extra (as prefix) besonders, extra, extra-, sonder-
eye Auge *n* das

F

fabric Stoff *m* der
face Gesicht *n* das
fact Tatsache *f* die
factory Fabrik *f* die
factual sachlich
fair gerecht
faithful treu
faithfulness Treue *f* die
fake Fälschung *f* die
fall fallen *V**, stürzen *V*; Herbst *m* der; Fall *m* der,
    Sturz *m* der
fall in love sich verlieben *V2*
false falsch, unecht, verkehrt
falsification Fälschung *f* die
familiar familiär
family Familie *f* die
famous berühmt
fantastic phantastisch, toll
fantasy Phantasie *f* die
far weit
far away weit weg
fare Fahrpreis *m* der, Preis *m* der
farm Bauernhof *m* der, Hof *m* der
farmer Bauer *m* der
farther weiter
fashion Mode *f* die
fast schnell
fastening Verschluß *m* der, Befestigung *f* die
fat Fett *n* das; Speck *m* der; fett, fettig
fatal tödlich; fatal
father Vater *m* der
faucet Hahn *m* der

faultless fehlerfrei, fehlerlos
favor Gefallen *m* der
fax Fax *n* das
fax machine Faxgerät *n* das
fear Furcht *f* die; Angst *f* die
feather Feder *f* die
February Februar *m* der
federation Verband *m* der, Vereinigung *f* die,
    Föderation *f* die
feed füttern *V*, ernähren *V2*
feel fühlen *V,* merken *V*
feel angry sich ärgern *V*
feel ashamed sich schämen *V*
feel like ... Lust haben *V* zu ...
feeling Gefühl *n* das
fellow Kerl *m* der
fence Zaun *m* der
festivity Fest *n* das, Feierlichkeit *f* die
fetch holen *V*
fever Fieber *n* das
few wenig, einige
fiancé Verlobte *m* der
fiancée Verlobte *f* die
field Feld *n* das
fight kämpfen *V,* streiten *V**; Kampf *m* der;
    Streit *m* der
fillet Filet *n* das
filling Füllung *f* die; (tooth) Plombe *f* die
film Film *m* der
filter Filter *m* der
filth Schmutz *m* der
filthy schmutzig
finally endlich
find finden *V**
fine fein, schön, gut; Strafe *f* die
finger Finger *m* der

finished fertig

fire Feuer *n* das

fire alarm Feueralarm *m* der

fire department Feuerwehr *f* die

fire extinguisher Feuerlöscher *m* der

fireworks Feuerwerk *n* das

firm Firma *f* die; fest

first erste *f*, erster *m*, erstes *n*; zuerst; **first floor**
Erdgeschoß *n* das

fish Fisch *m* der

fishbone Gräte *f* die

fit passen *V*

flag Fahne *f* die

flame Flamme *f* die

flat flach

flavor Geschmack *m* der

flee fliehen *V**

flight Flug *m* der

flirt flirten *V*

flood Flut *f* die

floor Boden *m* der

floppy disk Diskette *f* die

flour Mehl *n* das

flow fließen *V**

flower Blume *f* die

fluid flüssig

fly Fliege *f* die; fliegen *V**

foam Schaum *m* der

fog Nebel *m* der

follow folgen *V*; mitmachen *V1*

food Essen *n* das, Speise *f* die, Nahrung *f* die,
Lebensmittel *n/pl.* die

food store Lebensmittelgeschäft *n* das

foot Fuß *m* der, Bein *n* das

for für, denn

forbid verbieten *V**

forbidden verboten

force zwingen $V^\star$

forehead Stirn *f* die

foreign fremd

foreign country Ausland *n* das

foreigner Ausländer *m* der, Ausländerin *f* die, Fremder *m* der, Fremde *f* die

forest Wald *m* der

forever für immer

forget vergessen $V^\star 2$

forgive verzeihen $V^\star 2$; vergeben $V^\star 2$

fork Gabel *f* die

form Form *f* die

fortune Glück *n* das; Vermögen *n* das

foundation Stiftung *f* die

fourth Viertel *n* das

fragrance Duft *m* der

fraud Betrug *m* der

free frei, unentgeltlich, gratis; befreien *V2*

freedom Freiheit *f* die

freezer Tiefkühltruhe *f* die

freight Fracht *f* die

fresh frisch, kühl

freshwater Süßwasser *n* das

Friday Freitag *m* der

fridge Kühlschrank *m* der

friend Freund *m* der, Freundin *f* die

frighten erschrecken $V^\star 2$, Angst machen *V*

from von, aus, ab

from ~ on ab, von ~ ab

from the beginning von vorn, von vorne

from there von dort, dorther, daher

from this/that davon

from what woraus

from where woher

front Vorderseite *f* die, Vorder-; (in front) vorne;
  (in front of) vor
fruit Frucht *f* die, Obst *n* das
frying pan Pfanne *f* die
full voll
fun Spaß *m* der
function funktionieren *V2*, wirken *V*
funny lustig, komisch
fur Pelz *m* der, Fell *n* das
furnish einrichten *V1*
furniture Möbel *n* das
further weiter
fury Wut *f* die
future Zukunft *f* die
future tense Futur *n* das

G
gain verdienen *V2*
game Spiel *n* das; Wild *n* das
garbage Müll *m* der
garden Garten *m* der
gas Benzin *n* das; Gas *n* das
gasoline Benzin *n* das
gas station Tankstelle *f* die
gate Tor *n* das
gateway Tor *n* das
gay schwul
gears, gear unit Getriebe *n* das
general allgemein; **in general** im Allgemeinen
generation Generation *f* die
gentle sanft
genuine echt, original; **not genuine** unecht
germ Bakterie *f* die
get bekommen *V*2, holen *V,* fassen *V*; **get angry**
  sich ärgern *V*; **get up** aufstehen *V*1
giddy schwindelig

gift Geschenk *n* das

girl Mädchen *n* das

girlfriend Freundin *f* die

give geben *V**; (a gift) schenken *V*; **give away** vergeben *V*2*; **give back** wiedergeben *V*1*

gladly gern, gerne

gladness Freude *f* die

glass Glas *n* das

glasses (eye) Brille *f* die

glitter glänzen *V*

gloomy dunkel

go fahren *V**, gehen *V**

go ahead! los!

go along mitgehen *V*1*

go away fortgehen *V*1*, fortfahren *V*1*

go back zurückgehen *V*1*

go for a trip verreisen *V2*

go for a walk spazierengehen *V*1*

go out ausgehen *V*1*

go shopping einkaufen gehen

goal Tor *n* das; Ziel *n* das

god Gott *m* der

gold Gold *n* das

golden golden

gone fort, weg

good gut

Good-bye! Auf Wiedersehen!

Good morning! Guten Morgen!

Good night! Gute Nacht!

government Regierung *f* die

grade Grad *m* der, Stufe *f* die; Klasse *f* die; Steigung *f* die

grain Getreide *n* das, Korn *n* das

gram Gramm *n* das

grammar Grammatik *f* die

grandchild Enkel *m* der
grandparents Großeltern *f/pl.* die
grass Graß *n* das, Rasen *m* der
gratis gratis, unentgeltlich
gratitude Dank *m* der
gravity Schwerkraft *f* die
greasy fettig
great groß; toll, großartig
green grün
greet grüßen *V*
greeting Gruß *m* der
grill grillen *V,* braten *V**
grilled gegrillt, geröstet, gebraten
grocery Lebensmittelgeschäft *n* das
groom Bräutigam *m* der
gross brutto
ground Feld *n* das; Grund *m* der
grow wachsen *V**
grown-up erwachsen
growth Wachstum *n* das
guarantee garantieren *V2*; Garantie *f* die
guard beschützen *V,* schützen *V*
guess raten *V**, erraten *V*2*; Vermutung *f* die
guest Gast *m* der
guide führen *V;* Führer *m* der; Reiseführer *m* der
guidebook Reiseführer *m* der
guilt Schuld *f* die
guilty schuldig
guitar Gitarre *f* die
gulp Schluck *m* der
gun Pistole *f* die
gut Darm *m* der
guy Kerl *m* der
gymnastics Gymnastik *f* die
Gypsy Zigeuner *m* der

H

habit Gewohnheit *f* die, Sitte *f* die, Angewohnheit *f* die
habitual gewohnt
hair Haar *n* das
haircut Haarschnitt *m* der
hairdresser Friseur *m* der
hairdryer Fön *m* der
hairstyle Frisur *f* die
half halb; Hälfte *f* die
ham Schinken *m* der
hand Arm *m* der, Hand *f* die
handicap Behinderung *f* die
handicapped behindert; Behinderte *m* der,
    Behinderte *f* die
handkerchief Taschentuch *n* das
handwriting Schrift *f* die
handy praktisch
hangover Kater *m* der
happen passieren *V2*, geschehen *V*2*
happiness Glück *n* das, Freude *f* die
happy glücklich
harbor Hafen *m* der
hard hart; schwierig, schwer
hardness Härte *f* die
hardware Hardware *f* die
harm schaden *V*; Schaden *m* der, Verletzung *f* die
harmful schädlich
harmless harmlos, ungefährlich
harvest Ernte *f* die
haste Eile *f* die
hasty eilig
hate hassen *V*; Haß *m* der
have haben *V*
have influence Einfluß haben *V*; gelten *V**
have to müssen *V**
he er

head Kopf *m* der, Haupt *n* das, Spitze *f* die; Haupt-

heal heilen *V*, verheilen *V2*

health Gesundheit *f* die

health insurance Krankenkasse *f* die

healthy gesund

hear hören *V*

heart Herz *n* das

heat Hitze *f* die

heaven Himmel *m* der

heavy schwer

height Höhe *f* die; Größe *f* die

hello hallo

help helfen *V**; Hilfe *f* die

hemisphere Halbkugel *f* die

hence deshalb, daher

herb Kraut *n* das; **herbs** Kräuter *n/pl.* die

here hier, da, dort; hierher, hierhin, dorthin

heritage Erbe *n* das

hero Held *m* der

herself selbst, selber, sie selbst, alleine; *refl. pron.* sich

high hoch

higher höher

High German Hochdeutsch *n* das

high school Mittelschule *f* die, Realschule *f* die

high tide Flut *f* die

highway Autobahn *f* die

hike Wanderung *f* die; wandern *V*

hill Hügel *m* der, Berg *m* der

himself selbst, selber, er selbst, alleine; *refl. pron.* sich

hinder behindern *V2*

hire mieten *V*

hired car Mietwagen *m* der

his sein

history Geschichte *f* die

hit schlagen *V**, treffen *V**, stoßen *V**; Schlag *m* der, Stoß *m* der

hog Schwein *n* das

hold fassen *V,* halten *V**; Halt *m* der, Griff *m* der

hole Loch *n* das

holiday Urlaub *m* der

holidays Ferien *pl.* die

holiday apartment Ferienwohnung *f* die

holiday season Ferienzeit *f* die

holy heilig

home Heim *n* das, Haus *n* das, Zuhause *n* das, Heimat *f* die; nach Hause

honest ehrlich

honor Ehre *f* die

hook Haken *m* der

hope hoffen *V;* Hoffnung *f* die

horse Pferd *n* das

hospital Krankenhaus *n* das, (Austria, Switzerland) Spital *n* das

host Wirt *m* der; Wirtin *f* die; Gastgeber *m* der

hostile feindlich

hot heiß; (spicy) scharf

hotel Hotel *n* das

hour Stunde *f* die

house Haus *n* das

how wie

however doch, jedenfalls

hug umarmen *V2*; Umarmung *f* die

humid feucht

humidity Feuchtigkeit *f* die

hunger Hunger *m* der

hungry hungrig

hurricane Orkan *m* der

hurry Eile *f* die

hurt weh tun *V**, schmerzen *V*

husband Ehemann *m* der

I

I ich; **I myself** ich selber
ice Eis *n* das
ice cream Eis *n* das, Eiscreme *f* die
idea Idee *f* die
identity card Ausweis *m* der, Personalausweis *m* der
if wenn, ob
ill krank
illegal illegal
imagine sich etwas vorstellen *V1*
immediately sofort, unverzüglich, augenblicklich
immigrant Einwanderer *m* der
immoral unmoralisch
immortal unsterblich
impatient ungeduldig
impertinent unverschämt
import Einfuhr *f* die, Import *m* der; importieren *V2*
important wichtig
impossible unmöglich
impression Eindruck *m* der
improve verbessern *V2*
impudent unverschämt
in in, innen, hinein
in a hurry eilig
in a jumble durcheinander
in advance im voraus
in any case sowieso
in front of vor
in love verliebt
in order to um zu
in return dafür
in spite of trotz
in the evening abends
in the middle of mitten, inmitten
in transit in Transit, unterwegs
in what worin

in which worin
incalculable unberechenbar
incapable unfähig
income Einkommen *n* das
income tax Einkommensteuer *f* die
inconstant unbeständig
independent frei, unabhängig, selbständig
indicate zeigen *V*
industrial industriell
industrial area Industriegebiet *n* das
industry Industrie *f* die, Brache *f* die
informal unverbindlich
ingenious genial
inhabit bewohnen *V2*
inhabitant Einwohner *m* der
inherit erben *V*
initiation Einführung *f* die
injection Injektion *f* die, Spritze *f* die
injure schaden *V*
injurious schädlich
ink Tinte *f* die
innocence Unschuld *f* die
innocent unschuldig
inquire untersuchen *V2,* forschen *V*
inquiry Untersuchung *f* die; Frage *f* die
insect Insekt *n* das
insensible unempfindlich
inside innen, drinnen, in Innern
insignificant unwichtig
install einrichten *V1*
installation Installation *f* die; Einrichtung *f* die
instantly sofort, augenblicklich
instead (of) anstatt, anstelle von, dafür
institution Institution *f* die, Einrichtung *f* die
instruct unterrichten *V2*
instruction Unterricht *m* der

instrument Apparat *m* der, Instrument *n* das

insurance Versicherung *f* die; (health)
Krankenkasse *f* die

insured versichert

intellect Verstand *m* der

intellectual geistig

intelligent klug, intelligent

interesting interessant

intermission Pause *f* die

international international

international call Auslandsgespräch *n* das

interrupt unterbrechen *V**2

interruption Unterbrechung *f* die

intestines Darm *m* der

into in, hinein, herein

intoxication Vergiftung *f* die; Rausch *m* der

introduce einführen *V1*; **introduce someone**
vorstellen *V1*

introduction Einführung *f* die, Einleitung *f* die

inundation Überschwemmung *f* die

invalid ungültig

invent erfinden *V**2

investigate untersuchen *V2*

investigation Untersuchung *f* die

iron Eisen *n* das

irregular unregelmäßig

irritate ärgern *V*, irritieren *V*

island Insel *f* die

it es

itself selbst, selber, alleine; *refl. pron.* sich

J

jacket Jacke *f* die

January Januar *m* der

je ..., desto ... the ..., the ...

Jew Jude *m* der

jewelry Schmuck *m* der

Jewish jüdisch

job Arbeitsplatz *m* der, Stellung *f* die, Beruf *m* der, Aufgabe *f* die

join verbinden *V**2; mitmachen *V1*

joke Scherz *m* der, Witz *m* der

journey Reise *f* die, Fahrt *f* die

joy Freude *f* die

judgement Urteil *n* das

juice Saft *m* der

July Juli *m* der

jump springen *V**

June Juni *m* der

jurist Jurist *m* der

just nur, bloß; recht, gerecht; gerade; **just now** geradeeben

justice Justiz *f* die

K

keen eifrig; begierig, scharf

keep halten *V**

kernel Kern *m* der

key Schlüssel *m* der; Taste *f* die

keyboard Tastatur *f* die

kill töten *V*

kilogram Kilo *n* das, Kilogramm *n* das

kilometer Kilometer *m* der

kind lieb; Art *f* die

kindergarten Kindergarten *m* der

king König *m* der

kiss Kuß *m* der; küssen *V*

kitchen Küche *f* die

knee Knie *n* das

knife Messer *n* das

knife, fork and spoon Besteck *n* das

knock klopfen *V*

know können V^*, kennen V^*, wissen V^*
known bekannt

L

lady Dame *f* die
lake See *m* der
lamb Lamm *n* das
land Land *n* das; landen *V*
landing Landung *f* die
landlord Vermieter *m* der, Wirt *m* der, Wirtin *f* die
language Sprache *f* die
large groß, breit
last letzte *f*, letzer *m*, letztes *n*
last name Familienname *m* der
late spät
later später, nachher
lateral seitlich, quer
lather Schaum *m* der
laugh lachen *V*
laundry Wäsche *f* die
lavatory Klo *n* das, Klosett *n* das
law Gesetz *n* das, Recht *n* das
lawyer Jurist *m* der
lazy faul
lead führen *V*
leader Führer *m* der, Aufführer *m* der
leaf Blatt *n* das
lean mager
learn lernen *V*
leather Leder *n* das
leave wegfahren V^*1
leave gehen V^*, verlassen V^*2, lassen *V*
left links, nach links; **to the left** nach links **on the left** links
left over übrig
leg Fuß *m* der, Bein *n* das

legal legal

leisure Freizeit *f* die

leisure wear Freizeitkleidung *f* die

lemon Zitrone *f* die

lend leihen *V*

lesson Lektion *f* die, Unterrichtsstunde *f* die; Stunde *f* die

lessons Unterricht *m* der

let lassen *V**; vermieten *V2*

lethal tödlich

letter Brief *m* der; Buchstabe *m* der

liberty Freiheit *f* die

lick lecken *V*

lie Lüge *f* die; lügen *V**; liegen *V**

lift heben *V**

light leicht; Licht *n* das

lightbulb Glühbirne *f* die

lighter Feuerzeug *n* das

lightning Blitz *m* der

like wie, als; gefallen *V*2*, mögen *V**

likewise gleichfalls

line Strich *m* der

liquid flüssig

liquor Schnaps *m* der

listen hören *V*, zuhören *V1*

little klein, wenig, gering; (a little bit) bißchen, ein

live Leben *n* das; leben *V*, wohnen *V*

live in bewohnen *V2*

load Fracht *f* die, Ladung *f* die

loan leihen *V**

lock schließen *V**, verschließen *V*2*, einschließen *V*1*; Schloß *n* das, Verschluß *m* der; **lock up** einschließen *V*1*

lodging Quartier *n* das

long lang, lange

long-distance call Ferngespräch *n* das
look aussehen *V*1*, schauen *V*
look after nachsehen *V*1*
look at anschauen *V1*, ansehen *V*1*
look for suchen *V*
loose locker
lose verlieren *V*2*
lost verloren
loud laut
love Liebe *f* die; lieben *V*
low niedrig
low tide Ebbe *f* die
luck Glück *n* das; **bad luck** Unglück *n* das,
    Pech *n* das
lucky glücklich
lunch Mittagessen *n* das
lung Lunge *f* die

M

machine Maschine *f* die
mad verrückt
magnificent großartig, wundervoll
magnify vergrößern *V2*
mail Post *f* die
mailbox Briefkasten *m* der
maintain unterhalten *V*2*
main wiring Stromleitung *f* die, Leitung *f* die
make tun, machen *V*
make angry ärgern *V*
make a sign ein Zeichen *m* geben *V**, winken *V**
makeup Schminke *f* die; **apply makeup** sich
    schminken *V*
male männlich
mall Kaufhaus *n* das, Warenhaus *n* das
man Mann *m* der, Mensch *m* der

manage verwalten *V2*; schaffen *V**, hinbekommen *V*2*

management Management *n* das, Leitung *f* die, Direktion *f* die

manager Geschäftsführer *m* der, Manager *m* der

many viele

map Landkarte *f* die, Karte *f* die

March März *m* der

marriage Hochzeit *f* die, Ehe *f* die

married verheiratet

marry heiraten *V*

masculine männlich

match Streichholz *n* das

material Material *n* das, Stoff *m* der

matter Sache *f* die

May Mai *m* der

may dürfen *V**, können *V**; **may I?** Gestatten Sie?

maybe vielleicht

meadow Wiese *f* die

meager mager

meal Essen *n* das

mean bedeuten *V2*; gemein, böse

measure messen *V**; Maß *n* das

meat Fleisch *n* das

medicine Medizin *f* die, Medikament *n* das

meet treffen *V**

meeting point Treffpunkt *m* der

melody Melodie *f* die

memo Notiz *f* die

memory Gedächtnis *n* das

mental geistig

merchandise Ware *f* die

merchant Kaufmann *m* der, Händler *m* der

metal Metall *n* das

meter Meter *m* der

method Methode *f* die

metro S-Bahn *f* die, Metro *f* die

middle Mitte *f* die, Zentrum *n* das

might Macht *f* die

mighty mächtig

milk Milch *f* die

mind Seele *f* die

mine mein

mineral Mineral *n* das; **mineral oil** Erdöl *n* das

minimum mindestens

minister Minister *m* der

minute Minute *f* die

miracle Wunder *n* das

mirror Spiegel *m* der

misfortune Unglück *n* das

miss verpassen *V2*

Miss Fräulein *n* das; (followed by a name) Frau ...

mission Auftrag *m* der, Mission *f* die

mistake Fehler *m* der, Versehen *n* das; **by mistake** aus Versehen

Mister Herr *m* der; (followed by a name) Herr ~

mix mischen *V*; Mischung *f* die

mixed gemischt; **mixed up** durcheinander

modern modern

modest bescheiden

modesty Bescheidenheit *f* die; Scham *f* die

moist feucht

moment Moment *m* der

Monday Montag *m* der

money Geld *n* das; **to change money** Geld wechseln *V*

monetary transactions Geldgeschäfte *n/pl.* die

month Monat *m* der

mood Stimmung *f* die

moon Mond *m* der

moral Moral *f* die; moralisch

more mehr; **no more** nicht mehr

more than mehr als

morning Morgen *m* der, Vormittag *m* der; **in the morning** morgens, am Morgen

mosquito Mücke *f* die

most meist, meistens

mother Mutter *f* die

motion picture Spielfilm *m* der

motive Grund *m* der, Motiv *n* das

motor Motor *m* der

motorbike Motorrad *n* das

mountain Berg *m* der

mountain-railway Bergbahn *f* die

mountains Gebirge *n* das

mouth Mund *m* der

move bewegen *V2*; umziehen *V*1*; Umzug *m* der

movie Spielfilm *m* der, Film *m* der; **movies** Kino *n* das

Mr. Herr *m* der

Mrs. Frau *f* die; (followed by a name) Frau …

Ms. Fräulein *n* das

much viel

mud Schlamm *m* der, Dreck *m* der

multiple mehrfach

multitude Menge *f* die

murder Mord *m* der

murderer Mörder *m* der

muscle Muskel *m* der

mushroom Champignon *m* der, Pilz *m* der

music Musik *f* die

must müssen *V**, sollen *V*

mustard Senf *m* der

my mein

myself *refl. pron.* mich

mystery Geheimnis *n* das

N

name Name *m* der, Vorname *m* der; nennen *V**
namely nämlich
narrow eng, schmal
narrowness Enge *f* die
national national
native country Heimat *f* die
naturally natürlich
nature Natur *f* die
nausea Ekel *m* der; Übelkeit *f* die
near bei
nearly fast
neat sauber, hübsch, ordentlich
necessary nötig, notwendig
neck Hals *m* der
need brauchen *V*
needle Nadel *f* die
neither auch nicht
neither ... nor ... weder ... noch ...
net netto; Netz *n* das
never nie, niemals
never again nie wieder
nevertheless trotzdem
new neu
New Year's Day Neujahr *n* das
news Nachrichten *f/pl.* die
newspaper Zeitung *f* die
next nächster
nice nett, lieb
night Nacht *f* die
no nein, kein
noble edel
nobody keiner, niemand
noise Lärm *m* der
noisy laut

non- nicht, (as prefix) un-

none kein

nonflammable unbrennbar

non-transparent undurchsichtig

noon Mittag *m* der

no one keiner

no parking Parkverbot *n* das

normally normalerweise

north Norden *m* der; nördlich

northeast Nordosten *m* der

northwest Nordwesten *m* der

nose Nase *f* die

not nicht

not any kein

not at all überhaupt nicht

not dangerous ungefährlich

note Notiz *f* die; Note *f* die; beachten *V2*

nothing nichts

notice bemerken *V2*, merken *V,* beachten *V2*;
Nachricht *f* die

notify mitteilen *V1*

nourish nähren *V*, ernähren *V2*

novel Roman *m* der

November November *m* der

now nun

nude nackt

null Null *f* die

number Nummer *f* die, Zahl *f* die

nurse Krankenschwester *f* die

nut Nuß *f* die

nutrition Ernährung *f* die

O

oak Eiche *f* die

object Gegenstand *m* der; Zweck *m* der

obligation Verpflichtung *f* die, Pflicht *f* die; Schuld *f* die

obnoxious widerlich

observe beobachten *V2*, merken *V,* beachten *V2*

obvious klar, offensichtlich

occasion Gelegenheit *f* die

occupied belegt

ocean Meer *n* das, See *f* die

October Oktober *m* der

odd fremdartig

odor Geruch *m* der

of aus, von; **of the** *art.* des

off aus

offer anbieten *V*1*; Angebot *n* das

office Büro *n* das; Amt *n* das

officer Beamte *m* der; **police officer** Polizeibeamte *m* der, Polizist *m* der

often oft

oil Öl *n* das

ointment Salbe *f* die

old alt

olive Olive *f* die

on an, auf

on business geschäftlich

on top oben

on the way unterwegs

once einmal

one man

oneself *refl. pron.* sich

onion Zwiebel *f* die

only nur, erst, einzig

open geöffnet, offen

opera Oper *f* die

operate operieren *V2*, verkehren *V2*

operation Operation *f* die

opinion Meinung *f* die, Urteil *n* das

opponent Gegner *m* der

oppose sich widersetzen *V2*, ablehnen *V*

opposite Gegenteil *n* das

opposite side of gegenüber

oppress unterdrücken *V2*

or oder; **or ... or ...** entweder ... oder ...

orange Orange *f* die; orange

orange juice Orangensaft *m* der

order bestellen *V2*; Bestellung *f* die; Ordnung *f* die, Reihenfolge *f* die; **in order to** um zu

ordinary gewöhnlich

organ Organ *n* das

organism Organismus *m* der

organization Organisation *f* die

organize organisieren *V2*

original Original *n* das

orthography Rechtschreibung *f* die

other andere

other way round umgekehrt

otherwise andernfalls

our unser

ourselves *refl. pron.* uns

out aus, hinaus, heraus, außen

out of heraus, hinaus

out of order kaputt

out of reach unerreichbar

out of what woraus

outline Umriß *m* der

outside draußen, außen

oven Ofen *m* der

over über; mehr als

overhaul überholen *V2*, reparieren *V2*

overtake überholen *V2*

over there dort

overweight Übergewicht *n* das

owe schulden *V*

own besitzen *V**2; eigen
owner Inhaber *m* der
ox Ochse *m* der, Rind *n* das

P

pack pachen *V*, einpacken *V2*
package Paket *n* das, Päckchen *n* das
packet Paket *n* das
page Seite *f* die
pain Schmerz *m* der
painstaking fleißig
paint malen *V*; Farbe *f* die
painter Maler *m* der
pair Paar *n* das
pajamas Schlafanzug *m* der
pan Pfanne *f* die
pants Hose *f* die
paper Papier *n* das
paperbag Tüte *f* die, Papiertüte *f* die
paperback Taschenbuch *n* das
paprika Paprika *f* die
paraphrase umschreiben *V**2
parcel Paket *n* das
pardon verzeihen *V**2; Verzeihung *f* die
parents Eltern *pl.* die
park Park *m* der; (car) parken *V*
parking Parkplatz *m* der
parking lot Parkplatz *m* der
parliament Parlament *n* das
part Teil *m* der, Teil *n* das
party Party *f* die, Fest *n* das
pass passieren *V2*, überholen *V2*
passenger Passagier *m* der
passion Leidenschaft *f* die
passionate leidenschaftlich, temperamentvoll
passport Reisepaß *m* der, Paß *m* der, Ausweis *m* der

past Vergangenheit *f* die; vorbei
pasteboard Pappe *f* die
pastor Pfarrer *m* der
pastry shop Konditorei *f* die
past tense Imperfekt *n* das, Präteritum *n* das
patience Geduld *f* die
patient geduldig
pay bezahlen *V2*, zahlen *V*
payment Bezahlung *f* die
peace Frieden *m* der
peaceful friedlich
peach Pfirsich *m* der
pear Birne *f* die
pearl Perle *f* die
pediatrician Kinderarzt *m* der
peel Schale *f* die
pelt Fell *n* das
pen Stift *m* der
penalty Strafe *f* die
pencil Bleistift *m* der
peninsula Halbinsel *f* die
pension Gasthof *m* der, Pension *f* die; Rente *f* die
people Leute *pl.* die, Volk *n* das
pepper Pfeffer *m* der
percent Prozent *n* das
perceive erkennen *V*2*, wahrnehmen *V*1*
perfect perfekt
perfect tense Perfekt *n* das
perfume Parfüm *n* das
perhaps vielleicht
perish verderben *V*2*
permission Erlaubnis *f* die; **With your permission?** Gestatten Sie?
permit gestatten *V2*, lassen *V,* erlauben *V2*
person Person *f* die, Mensch *m* der
personally persönlich
personnel Personal *n* das

persuade überzeugen *V2*, überreden *V2*
persuasion Überzeugung *f* die
petrol Öl *n* das, Erdöl *n* das
pharmacy Apotheke *f* die
phone Telefon *n* das; anrufen *V1*, telefonieren *V2*
phone call Anruf *m* der
photograph Foto *n* das, Photo *n* das
phrase Satz *m* der
physical körperlich
piano Klavier *n* das
pick Pickel *m* der
picture Bild *n* das, Photo *n* das
pie Torte *f* die
piece Stück *n* das
piece of paper Zettel *m* der
pierce stechen *V**
pig Schwein *n* das
pigeon Taube *f* die
pile Stoß *m* der
pimple Pickel *m* der
pinch klauen *V*
pink rosa
pipe Rohr *n* das
pit Kern *m* der
pity Pech *n* das
place Platz *m* der, Stelle *f* die, Ort *m* der; stellen *V,* setzen *V*
plain flach; einfach
plan Plan *m* der
plane Fläche *f* die
plant Pflanze *f* die
plastic Plastik *n* das
plastic bag Plastiktüte *f* die
plate Teller *m* der
platform Gleis *n* das
play spielen *V*

please bitte, bitte sehr, bitte schön; gefallen V^*2
pleasure Vergnügen *n* das, Lust *f* die; **with pleasure** mit Vergnügen; **gladly** gern, gerne
plug Stecker *m* der
plum Pflaume *f* die
plunge Sturz *m* der
pluperfect Plusquamperfekt *n* das
plural Plural *m* der
pocket Tasche *f* die, Hosentasche *f* die
pocket calculator Taschenrechner *m* der
poet Dichter *m* der, Poet *m* der
point Punkt *m* der; Spitze *f* die
pointed spitz
poisonous giftig
police Polizei *f* die
policeman Polizist *m* der
polite höflich
politician Politiker *m* der
politics Politik *f* die
poor arm
popular beliebt, populär
pork Schweinefleisch *n* das
portion Portion *f* die
position Position *f* die, Lage *f* die; Stellung *f* die, Anstellung *f* die
possess besitzen V^*2
possession Besitz *m* der
possible möglich
post Post *f* die
postage Porto *n* das
post office Postamt *n* das, Post *f* die
potato Kartoffel *f* die
pound Pfund *n* das
pour schütten *V*, einschenken *V1*
pour out, pour in einschenken *V1*
power Macht *f* die, Kraft *f* die; Gewalt *f* die

powerful mächtig, stark, kräftig
practical praktisch
practice Praxis *f* die; üben *V*
praise loben *V*
pregnant schwanger
prefer vorziehen *V*1*, lieber + *verb*
premium gas Super *n* das, Superbenzin *n* das
prescription Vorschrift *f* die
present Geschenk *n* das; jetzig
present tense Präsens *n* das
president Präsident *m* der
press drücken *V*
pressure Druck *m* der
presume vermuten *V2*
pretty hübsch, schön
price Preis *m* der
priceless unbezahlbar
prick Stich *m* der; stechen *V**
priest Priester *m* der
prince Prinz *m* der, Fürst *m* der
principal Haupt-, Haupt *n* das, Chef *m* der, Leiter *m* der, Direktor *m* der
prison Gefängnis *n* das
private privat
privilege Recht *n* das
probably wahrscheinlich
process Prozeß *m* der
procession Umzug *m* der, Prozession *f* die
produce produzieren *V2*, schaffen *V**
profession Beruf *m* der
profit Nutzen *m* der
program Programm *n* das
prohibit verbieten *V**
prohibition Verbot *n* das
pronounce aussprechen *V*1*

pronunciation Aussprache *f* die
proof Beweis *m* der
prosperity Wohl *n* das
prostitute Prostituierte *f* die
prostitution Prostitution *f* die
protect beschützen *V,* schützen *V*
protection Schutz *m* der
protein Eiweiß *n* das
protest Protest *m* der; protestieren *V2*
proverb Sprichwort *n* das
province Provinz *f* die
proximity Nähe *f* die
proxy Vollmacht *f* die
public öffentlich
public baths Schwimmbad *n* das
publicity Reklame *f* die, Werbung *f* die
public servant Beamte *m* der
publisher Verlag *m* der
pull ziehen *V**
punishable strafbar
punishment Strafe *f* die
pupil Schüler *m* der, Schülerin *f* die
purchase Einkauf *m* der
pure rein
purpose Zweck *m* der
purse Geldbörse *f* die, Geldbeutel *m* der
pursue verfolgen *V2*
pursuit Fortsetzung *f* die, Verfolgung *f* die
push drücken *V,* stoßen *V**; Stoß *m* der
put legen *V,* stellen *V,* setzen *V*
put in order ordnen *V*

Q

quantity Menge *f* die
quarrel streiten *V**; Streit *m* der

question Frage *f* die
quick schnell
quiet still, ruhig; ziemlich
quotation Kurs *m* der

R

radio Radio *n* das
rage Wut *f* die
railroad Eisenbahn *f* die
railway station Bahnhof *m* der
rain Regen *m* der; regnen *V*
raise heben *V**
rate Kurs *m* der, Tarif *m* der
rational vernünftig
raw roh
razor Rasierapparat *m* der
razor blade Rasierklinge *f* die
react reagieren *V2*
reaction Reaktion *f* die
read lesen *V**
ready fertig, bereit
real wirklich, echt
really wirklich
reason Grund *m* der; Verstand *m* der,
    Vernunft *f* die
reasonable vernünftig
receive bekommen *V*2*, empfangen *V*2*
receiver Empfänger *m* der; Telefonhörer *m* der
reception Empfang *m* der
recipe Rezept *n* das
recognize erkennen
recollection Erinnerung *f* die
record Urkunde *f* die
recover sich erholen *V2*
recovery Erholung *f* die
red rot

reduce reduzieren *V2*, verkleinern *V2*
reflect überlegen *V2*, nachdenken *V*1*
reflection Überlegung *f* die
refrigerator Kühlschrank *m* der
refusal Ablehnung *f* die
region Region *f* die, Bezirk *m* der, Gegend *f* die
regret bedauern *V2*
regular regelmäßig
rehearsal Probe *f* die
related verwandt
relation Verhältnis *n* das, Beziehung *f* die
relationship Verhältnis *n* das, Beziehung *f* die
relative Verwandte *m* der, Verwandte *f* die
relax entspannen *V2*
relaxation Entspannung *f* die
relaxed locker
relevant sachlich, relevant
reliable zuverlässig
religion Religion *f* die
religious religiös, geistlich
remain bleiben *V**, übrigbleiben *V1*
remainder Rest *m* der
remaining übrig
remedy Gegenmittel *n* das
remember sich erinnern *V2*
remembrance Erinnerung *f* die, Gedächtnis *n* das
removal Umzug *m* der
rent Miete *f* die; mieten *V*; vermieten *V2*
rental car Mietwagen *m* der
repair Reparatur *f* die; reparieren *V2*
repeat wiederholen *V2*
repeated mehrfach, wiederholt
repetition Wiederholung *f* die
replace ersetzen *V2*
report melden *V*; Meldung *f* die, Nachricht *f* die
reproduce wiedergeben *V*1*, reproduzieren *V2*

republic Republik *f* die
request Bitte *f* die, Anfrage *f* die; bitten *V**
require benötigen *V2*, fordern *V*
required notwendig, nötig
rescue Rettung *f* die; retten *V*
research Suche *f* die
researcher Forscher *m* der
reserve Reserve *f* die; reservieren *V2*
reserved belegt
residence Aufenthalt *m* der, Wohnsitz *m* der
residence permit Aufenthaltsgenehmigung *f* die
residential area Wohngebiet *n* das
responsibility Verantwortung *f* die
responsible verantwortlich
rest sich ausruhen *V1*; Ruhe *f* die; Rest *m* der
restaurant Restaurant *n* das, Wirtschaft *f* die
result Ergebnis *n* das
return umdrehen *V1*, umkehren *V1*, zurückgehen
    *V*1*; wiedergeben *V*1*; wiederkommen *V*1*;
    Rückfahrt *f* die
return ticket Rückfahrkarte *f* die
reunification Wiedervereinigung *f* die
revenue office Finanzamt *n* das
reverse umgekehrt, umgekehrt
review Kritik *f* die, Besprechung *f* die
revolution Revolution *f* die
ribbon Band *n* das
rice Reis *m* der
rich reich
ride fahren *V**; Fahrt *f* die
right korrekt, richtig, recht, Recht *n* das; (on the
    right) rechts; (to the right) nach rechts, rechts
ring Ring *m* der; klingeln *V*
risk Risiko *n* das
river Fluß *m* der, Strom *m* der
road Straße *f* die

roast braten V^*

roasted gebraten

roast pork Schweinebraten *m* der

rob berauben *V2*

rock Fels *m* der

roll Brötchen *n* das, Semmel *f* die; rollen *V*

romantic romantisch

roof Dach *n* das

room Zimmer *n* das, Raum *m* der

rooster Hahn *m* der

root Wurzel *f* die

rope Seil *n* das

rose Rose *f* die

rot verderben V^*2

rotten faul, faulig, verfault

rouge Schminke *f* die

round rund

rudder Ruder *n* das, Steuer *n* das

ruin Untergang *m* der

rule Regel *f* die

rules Ordnung *f* die

run laufen V^*

rye Roggen *m* der

S

sacred heilig

sad traurig

safe sicher; Safe *m* der

safety Sicherheit *f* die

sailboat Segelboot *n* das

salad Salat *m* der

salary Gehalt *n* das

sales clerk Verkäufer *m* der, Verkäuferin *f* die

saliva Speichel *m* der, Spucke *f* die

salmon Lachs *m* der

saloon Wirtschaft *f* die, Kneipe *f* die

salt Salz *n* das
saltshaker Salzstreuer *m* der
salt water Salzwasser *n* das
salutation Gruß *m* der
salve Salbe *f* die
same selbe, gleiche
sand Sand *m* der
sanitary napkin Damenbinde *f* die
Saturday Samstag *m* der
sauce Soße *f* die
sauerkraut Sauerkraut *n* das
sauna Sauna *f* die
sausage Wurst *f* die
save retten *V*; sparen *V*
saving sparsam
say sagen *V*
saying Sprichwort *n* das
scale Skala *f* die; Schuppe *f* die
scare erschrecken *V*2*, Angst machen *V*
scene Szene *f* die
scent Duft *m* der, Geruch *m* der
school Schule *f* die
scientist Forscher *m* der
scissors Schere *f* die
scrambled eggs Rührei *n* das
screw Schraube *f* die
sea Meer *n* das, See *f* die
search suchen *V*, forschen *V*; Suche *f* die
seaside Meer *n* das
second Sekunde *f* die; zweite; (next one after)
   übernächste
secondary school Gymnasium *n* das
secret geheim; Geheimnis *n* das
secure sicher
security Sicherheit *f* die
see schauen *V*, sehen *V**

see again wiedersehen *V*1*
seed Samen *m* der
seek suchen *V*
seem scheinen *V**
seize fassen *V*
seldom selten
self selbst
self-employed selbständig
sell verkaufen *V2*
sensation Gefühl *n* das; Sensation *f* die
sense Sinn *m* der
sensitive empfindlich, sensibel
sentence Satz *m* der; Strafe *f* die
separate trennen *V*
September September *m* der
serious ernst, ernsthaft; seriös
service Bedienung *f* die, Service *m* der; überholen *V2*
serving Portion *f* die
set stellen *V*
settlement Abschluß *m* der
shack Hütte *f* die
shadow Schatten *m* der
shake schütteln *V,* zittern *V*
shall sollen
shallow flach
shame Scham *f* die
shameless schamlos
shape Form *f* die
share teilen *V*
sharp scharf
shave sich rasieren *V2*
she sie
shed Stall *m* der
sheet Blatt *n* das, Scheibe *f* die
shelf Fach *n* das
shell Schale *f* die

shine scheinen $V^\star$, leuchten V, glänzen V

ship Schiff n das

shirt Hemd n das

shit Scheiße f die (vulgar)

shiver zittern V

shock Schreck m der

shoe Schuh m der

shoemaker Schuster m der

shoot schießen $V^\star$

shop Geschäft n das, Laden m der; einkaufen gehen $V^\star$

shopping Einkauf m der

shopping center, shopping mall Kaufhaus n das, Warenhaus n das

shore Ufer n das

short kurz

shot Schuß m der

shout schreien $V^\star$

show zeigen V

shower Dusche f die; duschen V

shuffle mischen V

shut schließen $V^\star$, zumachen $V1$

sick krank, schlecht, übel

sickness Krankheit f die, Übelkeit f die

side Seite f die

side dish Beilage f die

sign Schild n das

signify bedeuten $V2$

silence Ruhe f die

silent leise

silk Seide f die

silly doof

silver Silber n das

similar ähnlich

similarity Ähnlichkeit f die

simple einfach

simplify vereinfachen *V2*

simultaneously gleichzeitig

sin Sünde *f* die

since seit; da, weil

sincere ehrlich

sinew Sehne *f* die

sing singen *V**

single einzig, einzeln, einfach; unverheiratet

singular Einzahl *f* die, Singular *m* der

sip Schluck *m* der

sir Herr *m* der

sister Schwester *f* die

sister-in-law Schwägerin *f* die

sit sitzen *V**, setzen *V*

sit down sich setzen *V*

sitting Sitzung *f* die

situation Lage *f* die, Situation *f* die

size Größe *f* die

ski Schi *m* der

skilled fähig

skin Haut *f* die

skirt Rock *m* der

sky Himmel *m* der

slap Schlag *m* der; (slap in the face) Ohrfeige *f* die

slaughter schlachten *V*

sleep schlafen *V**; Schlaf *m* der

sleeper Schlafwagen *m* der

slice Scheibe *f* die

slight gering

slip Zettel *m* der

slow langsam

small klein, gering

small parcel Päckchen *n* das

smart klug, schlau

smell Geruch *m* der, Duft *m* der; riechen *V**

smile lächeln *V*; Lächeln *n* das

smoke Rauch *m* der; rauchen *V*
smooth glatt
smut Schmutz *m* der
snack Schnellimbiß *m* der
snake Schlange *f* die
snow Schnee *m* der; schneien *V*
snowball Schneeball *m* der
snowflake Schneeflocke *f* die
so so; **so that** so daß; **so far** soweit; **so much** soviel
soap Seife *f* die
sober nüchtern
soccer Fußball *m* der
social sozial
society Gesellschaft *f* die
sock Socke *f* die
socket Steckdose *f* die
soft weich, sanft; leise
software Software *f* die
soil Erde *f* die, Boden *m* der
sojourn Aufenthalt *m* der
soldier Soldat *m* der
sole einzig
solely nur
solid fest
some etwas, einige, ein wenig, irgend, irgendein
somebody jemand
somehow irgendwie
someone man; jemand, irgend jemand
something etwas
some time irgendwann
somewhere irgendwo
son Sohn *m* der
song Lied *n* das
soon bald
soot Ruß *m* der
sore wund

sorrow Trauer *f* die, Sorge *f* die
Sorry! Entschuldigung!; **I'm sorry!** Es tut mir leid!
sort Art *f* die, Sorte *f* die
soul Seele *f* die
sound Geräusch *n* das, Ton *m* der
soup Suppe *f* die
sour sauer
source Quelle *f* die
south südlich; Süden *m* der
southeast Südosten *m* der
southwest Südwesten *m* der
sovereign Herrscher *m* der, Fürst *m* der
space Platz *m* der, Raum *m* der; Weltall *f* das,
    Weltraum *m* der
spare time Freizeit *f* die
spasm Krampf *m* der
speak reden *V,* sprechen *V**
special besonders, speziell, (as prefix) sonder-
spectators Publikum *n* das, Zuschauer *m* der
speed Geschwindigkeit *f* die, Tempo *n* das
spend ausgeben *V*1*
sperm Samen *m* der, Sperma *n* das
spice Gewürz *n* das
spicy scharf, würzig
spider Spinne *f* die
spiritual geistlich
spit spucken *V*
spittle Speichel *m* der, Spucke *f* die
splendid großartig, ausgezeichnet
spoon Löffel *m* der
sporting sportlich
sports Sport *m* der
spray Spray *n* das
spring Frühling *m* der; Quelle *f* die
stable stabil; Stall *m* der
stack Stoß *m* der

staff Personal *n* das

stage Bühne *f* die

staircase Treppenhaus *n* das, Treppe *f* die

stairs Treppe *f* die

stamp Briefmarke *f* die; Stempel *m* der

stand stehen *V**

stand up aufstehen *V*1*

star Stern *m* der

start anfangen *V*1*; Anfang *m* der, Start *m* der

state Staat *m* der

station Bahnhof *m* der, Station *f* die

statute Gesetz *n* das

stay bleiben *V**; Aufenthalt *m* der

stay overnight übernachten *V2*

steal klauen *V*

steel Stahl *m* der

steep steil

steering wheel Steuerrad *n* das, Steuer *n* das

step Schritt *m* der, Stufe *f* die; treten *V**

stick Stock *m* der

stiff steif

still noch

sting Stich *m* der, Stachel *m* der; stechen *V**

stink stinken *V**

stir rühren *V*

stock Vorrat *m* der

Stock Exchange Börse *f* die

stomach Magen *m* der

stomachache Magenschmerzen *m/pl.* die

stone Stein *m* der

stop Halt *m* der

stopover Zwischenlandung *f* die

store Laden *m* der, Geschäft *n* das

storm Sturm *m* der

story Geschichte *f* die

straight gerade
straight ahead geradeaus
strange fremd, fremdartig
stranger Fremder *m* der, Fremde *f* die
straw Stroh *n* das; **drinking straw** Strohhalm *m* der
strawberry Erdbeere *f* die
street Straße *f* die
strength Kraft *f* die, Stärke *f* die
stretch Strecke *f* die
strike Streik *m* der
stroke Strich *m* der
strong stark, kräftig
student Student *m* der
study lernen *V,* studieren *V2*; **studies** Studien *f/pl.* die
stuff Zeug *n* das
stupid dumm, doof, blöd
style Stil *m* der
subject Thema *n* das, Fach *n* das
substantive Substantiv *n* das
subtle fein
suburb Vorort *m* der
subway U-Bahn *f* die
succeed folgen *V,* gelingen *V*2*
success Erfolg *m* der
such solch, so ein
suddenly plötzlich
sue verklagen *V2*
suffer leiden
sugar Zucker *m* der
suit Klage *f* die; Anzug *m* der
suitcase Koffer *m* der
sultry schwül
summer Sommer *m* der
sun Sonne *f* die
sunbathe sich sonnen *V*

Sunday Sonntag *m* der

sunrise Sonnenaufgang *m* der

sunset Sonnenuntergang *m* der

suntan Bräune *f* die

supervise überwachen *V2*

supervision Kontrolle *f* die, Überwachung *f* die

supplies Proviant *m* der

suppose vermuten *V2*

suppress unterdrücken *V2*

sure sicherlich

surely sicherlich, bestimmt

surface Fläche *f* die

surgery Operation *f* die

surname Nachname *m* der, Familienname *m* der

surprise überraschen *V2*; Überraschung *f* die

surroundings Umgebung *f* die

survey Übersicht *f* die

survive überleben *V2*

suspect verdächtig

suspicion Verdacht *m* der

swear fluchen *V*

swearword Fluch *m* der

sweat Schweiß *m* der; schwitzen *V*

sweater Pullover *m* der

sweatshirt Pullover *m* der

sweet süß; niedlich, hübsch; Bonbon *n* das,
Süßigkeit *f* die

swim schwimmen *V**

swimming pool Schwimmbecken *n* das,
Schwimmbad *n* das

switch schalten *V*; Schalter *m* der

switch off ausschalten *V1*

syllable Silbe *f* die

symbol Symbol *n* das

sympathetic sympathisch

sympathy Sympathie *f* die
synagogue Synagoge *f* die
syringe Spritze *f* die

T

table Tisch
tableware Geschirr *n* das
tact Takt *m* der
tail Schwanz *m* der
tailor Schneider *m* der
take nehmen *V**, bringen *V**
take along mitnehmen *V*1*
take a seat sich setzen *V*
take away mitnehmen *V*1*
take-off Start *m* der, Abflug *m* der
take over übernehmen *V*2*
take place passieren *V2*, stattfinden *V*1*,
    geschehen *V*2*; sich setzen *V*
tale Geschichte *f* die
talk Gespräch *n* das
tall groß
tampon Tampon *m* der
tank Panzer *m* der; Tank *m* der
target Ziel *n* das
tariff Tarif *m* der
task Aufgabe *f* die
taste probieren *V2*, kosten *V*, schmecken *V*,
    versuchen; Geschmack *m* der
tattoo Tätowierung *f* die
tax Steuer *f* die
taxi Taxi *n* das
tea Tee *m* der
teach lehren *V*, unterrichten *V2*
teacher Lehrer *m* der
tear Träne *f* die
technical technisch

technique Technik *f* die
technology Technik *f* die, Technologie *f* die
telegram Telegramm *n* das
telephone Telephon *n* das
telephone conversation Telefongespräch *n* das
telephone directory Telefonbuch *n* das
television Fernseher *m* der
tell erzählen *V2*
temper Temperament *n* das
temperament Temperament *n* das
temperature Temperatur *f* die
tempo Tempo *n* das
tender zart
tenderly zärtlich
tennis Tennis *n* das
tension Spannung *f* die
tent Zelt *n* das
terminate enden *V*
terrace Terrasse *f* die
terror Schreck *m* der
test testen *V*; Test *m* der
testament Testament *n* das
text Text *m* der
than als, denn
thank danken *V*
thank you danke; **Thank you!** Vielen Dank!
    thanks! danke! Vielen Dank!
thanks Dank *m* der
that daß; das, dies, diese *f*, dieser *m*, dieses *n*; **so**
    that so daß
that is nämlich
the *art.* das, der, die
theater Theater *n* das
themselves selbst, selber, alleine; *refl. pron.* sich
then dann; damals
theoretical theoretisch

theory Theorie *f* die

there da, dort; dahin, dorthin

therefore deshalb, daher; also

thermal spa Thermalbad *n* das

thermal spring Thermalquelle *f* die

thick dick

thief Dieb *m* der

thin dünn

thing Ding *n* das, Sache *f* die

think denken *V**, glauben *V*, überlegen *V2*

thirst Durst *m* der

thirsty durstig

thought Gedanke *m* der

thread Faden *m* der

thrilling spannend, aufregend

throat Kehle *f* die, Hals *m* der

through durch

throw werfen *V**

throw away wegwerfen *V*1*

throw up brechen *V**, erbrechen *V*2*

thumb Daumen *m* der

thunder Donner *m* der

thunderstorm Gewitter *n* das, Unwetter *n* das

Thursday Donnerstag *m* der

thus also, daher

ticket Ticket *n* das; Karte *f* die, Eintrittskarte *f* die, Fahrkarte *f* die

ticket office Kartenschalter *m* der

tickle kitzeln

tide Flut *f* die; **low tide, ebb tide** Ebbe *f* die; **high tide** Flut *f* die

tidy ordentlich, aufgeräumt

tightness Enge *f* die

till bis

time Zeit *f* die, Uhrzeit *f* die

times -mal; **three times** dreimal; **ten times** zehnmal

timetable Fahrplan *m* der

tire Reifen *m* der

title Titel *m* der

to zu, bis zu, an; **to the** zu dem, zum; **to you** dir, für dich, zu dir; euch, zu euch; **to whom** wem

toast Toast *m* der

tobacco Tabak *m* der

today heute

toe Zeh *f* der

together zusammen, gemeinsam

toilet Klo *n* das, Klosett *n* das

tomorrow morgen

ton (weight) Tonne *f* die

tone Ton *m* der

tongue Zunge *f* die

too auch; zu, allzu; **too little** zuwenig; **too much** zuviel

tool Instrument *n* das, Werkzeug *n* das, Gerät *n* das

tooth Zahn *m* der

top Spitze *f* die, Kopf *m* der

topic Thema *n* das, Gegenstand *m* der

total total

touch Gefühl *n* das; Berührung *f* die; anfassen *V1*, berühren *V2*

tour Tour *f* die, Reise *f* die

tourism Tourismus *m* der

tourist Tourist *m* der

towards in Richtung, nach, zu

towel Handtuch *n* das

tower Turm *m* der

toy Spielzeug *n* das

trade Handel *m* der, Brache *f* die; handeln *V*

trading commerce Handelsverkehr *m* der

traffic Verkehr *m* der
traffic jam Stau *m* der
train Zug *m* der
tramway Straßenbahn *f* die, Trambahn *f* die
transcribe umschreiben *V*1*
transfer umbuchen *V1*
transferable übertragbar *V*2*
transit Durchreise *f* die
translate übersetzen *V2*
translation Übersetzung *f* die
transportation Verkehr *m* der, Transport *m* der
travel Reise *f* die; reisen, verreisen *V2*
traveling salesman Geschäftsreisende *m* der
traverse quer
tree Baum *m* der
tremble zittern *V*
trial Versuch *m* der, Probe *f* die
trick Trick *m* der
trip Ausflug *m* der
trip abroad Auslandsreise *f* die
trouble Störung *f* die
trousers Hose *f* die
true wahr
trust vertrauen *V2*; Vertrauen *n* das
trustworthy seriös
truth Wahrheit *f* die, Treue *f* die
try testen *V,* probieren *V2*, versuchen *V2*
tube Rohr *n* das
Tuesday Dienstag *m* der
tumble stürzen *V*
tuna Thunfisch *m* der
turkey Truthahn *m* der
turn drehen *V,* umdrehen *V1*
turn back umdrehen *V1*, umkehren *V1*
turn upside down umdrehen *V1*

tuxedo Smoking *m* der
twice zweimal
twice as much doppelt so viel
twin Zwilling *m* der

U

under unter
underpants Unterhose *f* die
underpass Unterführung *f* die
undershirt Unterhemd *n* das
understand verstehen *V*2, können *V**, kapieren *V*2
undertake unternehmen *V**2, übernehmen *V**2
uneducated ungebildet
unfortunately leider
unhealthy ungesund
uninhabited unbewohnt
unintelligible unverständlich
union Verband *m* der, Vereinigung *f* die;
    Gewerkschaft *f* die
unite verbinden *V**2, vereinigen *V*2
united vereinigt, einig
universe Weltall *n* das, Weltraum *m* der
unknown unbekannt
unless außer wenn
unmarried unverheiratet
unnecessary überflüssig
unstable unbeständig
untalented unbegabt
until bis
up hinauf, aufwärts
upstairs oben, nach oben
up to bis
urgent dringend
urine Urin *m* der
us uns

use benutzen *V2*, nutzen *V*, gebrauchen *V2*, nützen
V; Gebrauch *m* der; Nutzen *m* der
use up verbrauchen *V2*, aufbrauchen *V1*

V

vacant frei
vacation Urlaub *m* der, Ferien *pl.* die
vacationer Urlauber *m* der
valid gültig
valley Tal *n* das
value Wert *m* der
valve Ventil *n* das
vase Vase *f* die
veal Kalbfleisch *n* das
vegetarian Vegetarier *m* der
vehement heftig
vehicle Wagen *m* der
ventilation Lüftung *f* die
verb Verb *n* das
verification Überprüfung *f* die
verify kontrollieren *V2*, verifizieren *V1*
very sehr
vessel Schiff *n* das; Geschirr *n* das
victory Sieg *m* der
view besichtigen *V2*
villa Villa *f* die
village Dorf
vineyard Weinberg *m* der
vintage Jahrgang *m* der
violence Gewalt *f* die
violent heftig
violin Geige *f* die
virtue Tugend *f* die
virus Virus *n* das
visa Visum *n* das
vis-à-vis gegenüber

viscera Eingeweide *n/pl.* die
visit besuchen *V2*, besichtigen *V2*; Besuch *m* der
visitor Gast *m* der
vivacious temperamentvoll
voice Stimme *f* die
voltage Spannung *f* die, Stromspannung *f* die
volume Band *m* der
vomit brechen *V**, erbrechen *V*2*
voyage Reise *f* die

W

wait warten *V*; Warten *n* das, Aufenthalt *m* der
waiter Kellner *m* der
waitress Kellnerin *f* die
wake up aufwecken *V1*, wecken *V*; aufwachen *V1*
walk gehen *V**, laufen *V**, spazieren *V2*;
　　Spaziergang *m* der; **walk on** weitergehen *V*1*
walkout Streik *m* der
wall Mauer *f* die, Wand *f* die
walnut Walnuß *f* die
waltz Walzer *m* der
wander wandern *V*
want wollen *V*, mögen *V**
war Krieg *m* der
ware Ware *f* die
warm warm
warmth Wärme *f* die
warn warnen *V*
warning Warnung *f* die
warrant garantieren *V2*
warranty Garantie *f* die
wash waschen *V**
waste Abfall *m* der
watch beobachten *V2*, anschauen *V1*, ansehen *V*1*;
　　Uhr *f* die
water Wasser *n* das

water pipes Wasserleitung *f* die
wave Welle *f* die; winken *V**
wax Wachs *n* das
way Straße *f* die, Weg *m* der; Methode *f* die, Art *f* die
weak schwach; Woche *f* die
weakness Schwäche *f* die
weak point Schwäche *f* die
weapon Waffe *f* die
weather Wetter *n* das
wedding Hochzeit *f* die
Wednesday Mittwoch *m* der
weight Gewicht *n* das
welcome willkommen; **You're welcome!** Nichts
   zu danken! Macht nicht!
welfare Wohl *n* das
well gut
well-known bekannt
west Westen *m* der; westlich
wet naß
what was; *rel. pron.* der *m*, die *f*, das *n*, welcher *m*,
   welche *f*, welches *n*
wheat Weizen *m* der
wheat beer Weißbier *n* das
wheel Rad *n* das
when wann; wenn; als
where wo, wohin
whether ob
which welcher *m*, welche *f*, welches *n*; *rel. pron.* der
   m, die *f*, das *n*
white weiß
white bread Weißbrot *n* das
white of egg Eiweiß *n* das
who wer; *rel. pron.* der *m*, die *f*, das *n*
whole ganz, gesamt
wholesale trade Großhandel *m* der
whole-wheat bread Vollkornbrot *n* das

whom wen; **to whom** wem

whose wessen

why warum

wife Ehefrau *f* die

wild wild

will Wille *m* der

win gewinnen *V*2*, siegen *V*

wind Wind *m* der

window Fenster *n* das

wine Wein *m* der

wine cellar Weinkeller *m* der

winegrower Winzer *m* der

winter Winter *m* der

wish wünschen *V*, wollen *V*; Wunsch *m* der

wit Witz *m* der

witch Hexe *f* die

with mit, bei

within in; innen

without ohne

woman Frau *f* die

wonder Wunder *n* das

wonderful wunderbar, wunderschön

wood Holz *n* das

word Wort *n* das

words Text *m* der

work Arbeit *f* die, Werk *n* das; arbeiten *V*, funktionieren *V2*, wirken *V*

work together zusammenarbeiten *V1*

working hours Arbeitszeit *f* die

world Welt *f* die

worm Wurm *m* der

worried besorgt

worth Wert *m* der; wert

wound verwunden *V2*

wounded wund

write schreiben $V^\star$
writer Autor *m* der, Schriftsteller *m* der
writing Schrift *f* die
wrong falsch, verkehrt

Y

year Jahr *n* das, Jahrgang *m* der
yeast Hefe *f* die
yell schreien $V^\star$, schreien $V^\star$, Schrei *m* der
yellow gelb
yes ja
yesterday gestern
yet doch, noch; **not yet** noch nicht
you du, dich; ihr, euch; (polite) Sie; **you yourself**
  du selber
young jung
your dein; euer; (polite) ihr
yours dein; euer
yourself *refl. pr.* dich
yourselves *refl. pr.* euch
youth Jugend *f* die

X

x-ray röntgen *V*; Röntgenstrahl *m* der

Z

zero Null *f* die
zoo Zoo *m* der

GERMAN PHRASEBOOK

➤ Meeting and Greeting

Guten Tag!
Hello!

Grüß Gott!
Hello!

Hallo!
Hi!

Guten Morgen!
Good morning!

Guten Abend!
Good evening!

Wie geht es Ihnen? (polite)
Wie geht es Dir? (familiar)
How are you?

Gut, danke!
Fine, thanks!

Und Ihnen? (polite) / **Und Dir?** (familiar)
And you?

Mir geht es auch gut, danke!
I'm fine, too, thanks!

Es freut mich, Sie kennenzulernen! (polite)
Ich freue mich, Dich kennenzulernen! (familiar)
Nice to meet you!

Auf Wiedersehen!
Good-bye!

Tschüß! (familiar)
See you! Bye!

Gute Reise!
Bon voyage!

Auf Wiederhören!
Good-bye! (on the telephone)

Kennen wir uns nicht von irgendwoher?
Didn't we meet before?

Wie geht es Ihrer Frau? / Ihrem Mann? / Ihrer Tochter?
How is your wife? / your husband? / your daughter?

Wie geht es Ihren Kindern? / Ihren Freunden?
How are your children? / your friends?

Es freut mich, Sie kennenzulernen! (polite)
Es freut mich, Dich kennenzulernen! (familiar)
Pleased / Nice to meet you!

Gute Nacht!
Good night!

Schlafen Sie gut! (polite)
Schlaf gut! (familiar)
Sleep well!

➤ Basic Words and Phrases

Ja
Yes

Nein
No

Entschuldigung!
Excuse me!, Sorry!

Entschuldigen Sie bitte! (formal, also used when asking for information)
Excuse me!

Sprechen Sie Englisch?
Do you speak English?

Ich spreche kein Deutsch!
I do not speak German!

Sprechen Sie bitte langsamer!
Please speak slower!

Danke / Vielen Dank
Thanks / Thank you

Bitte
Please

Darf ich?
May I?

Können Sie mir bitte helfen?
Could you help me please?

BASIC WORDS AND PHRASES

Ich verstehe Sie / Dich nicht!
I don't understand you! (polite/familiar)

Ich verstehe (nicht)!
I (don't) understand!

Was ist das?
What's that?

Wer ist das?
Who is this?

Wohin fährt dieser Bus?
Where does this bus go to?

Rechts / Nach rechts.
Right / To the right.

Links / Nach links.
Left / To the left.

Oben / Nach oben.
Above / Up.

Unten / Nach unten.
Down / Down.

Wieviel kostet das?
How much does this cost?

Wieviel Uhr ist es bitte?
What time is it please?

Wann kommt _____ an?
When does _____ arrive?

Wann fährt _____ ab?
When does _____ leave?

> **... der Bus ...**
> ... the bus ...

> **... die S-Bahn ...**
> ... the metro ...

> **... der Zug ...**
> ... the train ...

> **... die Straßenbahn ...**
> ... the tramway ...

Geöffnet / Geschlossen.
Open / Closed.

Ich würde gerne ...
I would like to ...

Ich hätte gerne ...
I would like to have ...

With your permission?
Gestatten Sie?

Ich brauche ...
I need ...

Geben Sie mir bitte ...
Please give me ...

Wie weit ist es bis ...
How far is it until ...

> **... München?**
> ... Munich?

... zum Bahnhof / Flughafen?
... to the railway station / airport?

... zur Straßenbahnhaltestelle?
... to the tramway station?

Wo ist ...
Where is ...

... ein Hotel?
... a hotel?

... die Toilette?
... the toilet?

Wie komme ich ...
How do I get ...

... in die _____ Straße?
... to the _____ street?

... zum Bahnhof / Flughafen?
... to the railway station / airport?

Colors

rot – red
grün – green
blau – blue
gelb – yellow
orange – orange
weiß – white
schwarz – black
lila – violet
rosa – pink

Quick Reference

I - **ich**
you *sg.* - **du** (familiar) / **Sie** (polite)
he - **er**
she - **sie**
it - **es**
we - **wir**
you *pl.* - **sie** (familiar) / **Sie** (polite)
they - **sie**

this - **dieser** *m* / **diese** *f* / **dieses** *n*
that - **jener** *m* / **jene** *f* / **jenes** *n*
these - **diese** *m/f/n*
those - **jene** *m/f/n*

here - **hier**
there - **dort**

where? - **wo?**
who? - **wer?**
what? - **was?**
which? - **welcher?** *m* / **welche?** *f* / **welches?** *n*
when? - **wann?**
how? - **wie?**
why? - **warum?**
how far? - **wie weit?**
how much? - **wieviel?**
how many? - **wieviele?**
where is ...? - **wo ist ...?**

and - **und**
or - **oder**
but - **aber**

➤ Directions

When asking for directions, the prepositions *nach* and *zu* are used. When referring to a country, a city, or a suburb, *nach* is used. *Zu* + article is used in all other cases. Note that the preposition merges with the following article.

Wie komme ich bitte nach _____?
How do I get to _____, please?

Wo ist bitte der / die / das _____?
Where is the _____, please?

Geradeaus.
Straight ahead.

Links / Nach links.
Left / To the left.

Rechts / Nach rechts.
Right / To the right.

Sie müssen nach links / rechts gehen!
You must turn left / right.

Zurück.
Backwards.

Oben / Unten
Up / Down, stairs: upstairs / downstairs

Die zweite / _____ Straße nach links / rechts.
After the second / _____ street turn left / right.

Norden
North

Süden
South

Osten
East

Westen
West

➤ Weather

Germany, Austria, and Switzerland have a moderate climate without extremely cold or hot periods. The winter in the Alps region does not usually reach the lows of an Alaskan winter, neither can summertime compare to a summer's day in Texas.

In Europe temperature is measured in degrees centigrade, not in Fahrenheit. The freezing point of water (32 F°) is 0 C°.

The conversion formulas from Fahrenheit to Celsius and vice versa are:

$$F° = 9/5 \ C° + 32$$
$$C° = 9/5 \ (F°\text{-}32)$$

Wie wird das Wetter heute werden?
What will the weather be today?

Die Sonne scheint.
The sun is shining.

Das Wetter ist ...
It is ...

> **... sonnig.**
> ... sunny.

> **... wolkig / bedeckt.**
> ... cloudy.

> **... gut / schlecht.**
> ... good / bad.

... regnerisch.
... rainy.

... nebelig.
... foggy.

... windig.
... windy.

... stürmisch.
... stormy.

Wird es ...
Will it ...

... regnen?
... be raining?

... schneien?
... be snowing?

... kalt?
... become cold?

... warm?
... become warm?

... heiß?
... become hot?

Wie sind die Aussichten? / Wie ist die Wetter-vorhersage?
How are the predictions? / How is the weather forecast?

Um wieviel Uhr wird es dunkel / hell?
At what time does it become dark / light?

Um wieviel Uhr ist der Sonnenaufgang / Sonnenuntergang?
At what time is sunset / sunrise?

Es gibt ein Gewitter.
We will have a thunderstorm.

Sturm - storm

Regen - rain

Wind - wind

Sonnenschein - sunshine

Gewitter - thunderstorm

Donner - thunder

Blitz - lightning

➤ Travel and Transportation

In European countries most distances can be traveled by car or train. Trains are inexpensive, safe, fast, and clean. You should not forget to reserve your seats in trains.

Cars can be rented at railway stations, airports, in big hotels and downtown in the cities. Rental agencies provide insurance against injuries to other persons or objects caused by the person who rents the car. This is called *Haftpflichtversicherung* (third-party insurance), and it is obligatory. For a little more one can also be insured against damages caused to the rental car. This is called *Kasko-Versicherung*. Two kinds of *Kasko* exist: *Vollkasko* (full *kasko*), and *Teilkasko* (partial *kasko*). *Vollkasko* means full coverage of damages to the rental car, while *Teilkasko*, that is cheaper, covers only damages that cost more than 200 or 300 DM (ca. 1,400 or 2,100 ATS / 200 or 300 SFr). Injuries or damage below this limit have to be paid by the person who rented the car, or who caused the injury. Note that gasoline is much more expensive in Europe than in the United States.

Public transportation in the cities is very convenient. Subways (the metro), tramways or buses are often faster than taxis. Taxis are also much more expensive than in the United States.

Wo ist die nächste S-Bahn-Haltestelle?
Where is the next metro stop?

Wo ist die nächste Straßenbahnhaltestelle / Bushaltestelle?
Where is the next tramway station / bus station?

TRAVEL & TRANSPORTATION

Wie komme ich mit öffentlichen Verkehrsmitteln nach / zu ____?
How do I get to ____ by public transportation?

Wo finde ich ein Reisebüro?
Where do I find a travel agency?

Ich möchte eine Reise / einen Flug / einen Ausflug nach ___ buchen.
I want to book a trip / a flight / an excursion to ____.

Ich möchte einen Sitzplatz reservieren.
I want to reserve a seat.

Am Fenster. / Am Gang.
By the window. / On the aisle.

Im Raucherabteil. / Im Nichtraucherabteil.
In a smoking compartment. / In a non-smoking compartment.

Wieviel kostet eine Fahrkarte nach ____?
How much is a ticket to ____?

Wieviel kostet eine Tageskarte?
How much is a day-ticket?

I möchte eine Fahrkarte nach ____!
I want a ticket to ____!

Wo ist bitte ...
Please, where is ...

    ... der Flughafen?
    ... the airport?

    ... der Bahnhof?
    ... the railway station?

Ich hätte gerne ein Taxi zum Flughafen / Bahnhof.
I'd like to have a taxi to the airport / railway station.

Bringen Sie mich bitte nach / zum _____!
Bring me to (the) _____, please!

Von wo geht der Flug nach _____?
From where does the flight to _____ depart?

Wie komme ich zu Ausgang _____?
How do I get to gate _____?

Von welchem Gleis fährt der Zug nach _____?
From which platform does the train to _____ leave?

Muß ich umsteigen?
Do I have to change?

Wo muß ich umsteigen?
Where do I have to change?

Ich hätte bitte eine Fahrkarte erster / zweiter Klasse nach _____.
I'd like to have a first / second class ticket to _____.

Hin und zurück.
Back and forth.

Ich möchte ein Auto mieten.
I'd like to rent a car.

Für 1 Tag / Für _____ Tage.
For 1 day / For _____ days.

Ich hatte einen Unfall.
I had an accident.

Ich brauche / Wir brauchen einen Kranken-wagen.
I need / We need an ambulance.

Ich brauche die Polizei.
I need the police.

Jemand ist verletzt!
Somebody is hurt.

Ich habe eine Panne.
My car broke down.

Ein Reifen ist kaputt.
A tire is flat.

Ich habe kein Benzin mehr.
I ran out of gasoline.

Ich brauche einen Abschleppwagen.
I need a tow truck.

Ich bin (nicht) versichert!
I am (not) insured!

Meine Versicherung bezahlt das (nicht)!
My insurance pays that (doesn't pay that)!

Customs

If a customs officer catches you smuggling you will not only have to pay the customs fee, but also a penalty that is at last twice as high as the customs fee.

At European airports you used to find Duty-Free Shops, where you could do tax-free shopping, especially for wine, liquor, tobacco, perfume, and other

luxury goods. Since the year 2000 these shops no
longer exist for inter-European flights. The shops are
still open, but the prices are only a little cheaper than
elsewhere.

Haben Sie etwas zu verzollen?
Do you have anything to declare?

Ich habe nichts / etwas zu verzollen!
I have nothing / something to declare.

Ich weiß nicht, ob das zollfrei ist!
I don't know if this is duty-free!

**Bitte öffnen Sie Ihren Koffer / Ihre Tasche / Ihr
Gepäck!**
Please open your suitcase / your bag / your luggage!

Ihren Paß / Ausweis, bitte!
Your passport / I.D. card, please!

➤ Accommodations

Good accommodations are generally easy to find in Europe. In cities you will find street signs helping you to locate the different types of accommodation. You will find hotels, *Hotels garni*, pensions, *Gästezimmer*, motels, youth hostels, and camping sites.

A hotel garni (*Hotel garni*) only serves breakfast. These hotels usually do not have a restaurant. Pensions offer two types of accommodation: full pension (*Vollpension*) and half pension (*Halbpension*). *Vollpension* includes three meals with the room (breakfast, lunch, and dinner), *Halbpension* includes breakfast and dinner only. Neither one includes drinks. *Gästezimmer* are rooms offered by persons in their private homes. These are usually very cheap, and sometimes you are included in family life. You are provided with breakfast at the least, and sometimes even lunch, dinner, and food supplies on your tours. Motels are not very common in Europe.

Youth hostels usually host only young people (until 28 years of age). They do not have hotel standards. Rooms usually have to be shared with other people. Meals are served, but have to be paid separately.

Camping sites are for trailers and tents. No meals are served, but most camping sites do have small shops. Showers can be used, but usually must be paid for separately.

Ich suche / Wir suchen ...
I am / We are looking for ...

>**... ein Hotel.**
>... a hotel.

ACCOMMODATIONS

... eine Pension.
... a pension.

... Fremdenzimmer.
... guest rooms.

... ein Motel.
... a motel.

... die Jugendherberge.
... the youth hostel.

... einen Campingplatz.
... a camping site.

Können Sie uns ein Hotel empfehlen?
Can you recommend a hotel?

Luxuskategorie.
Five-star hotel / Luxury hotel.

Mittlere Preisklasse.
Middle class hotel.

Ein preisgünstiges Hotel.
A cheap hotel.

Wie lange möchten Sie bleiben?
How long will you be staying?

Ich / Wir werden _____ Nächte bleiben.
I am / We are going to stay for _____ nights.

Ich möchte / Wir möchten ein Zimmer mit ...
I'd / We'd like to have a room with ...

Gibt es auch ein Zimmer mit ...
Do you have rooms with ...

> **... Dusche und Bad.**
> ... shower and bathroom.

> **... Fernseher.**
> ... TV.

> **... Telefon.**
> ... telephone.

> **... Aussicht.**
> ... a nice view.

Ich möchte ... / Wir möchten ...
I would like ... / We would like ...

> **... ein Einzelzimmer.**
> ... a single room.

> **... ein Doppelzimmer.**
> ... a double room.

> **... ein Nichtraucherzimmer.**
> ... a non-smoking room.

> **... ein Raucherzimmer.**
> ... a smoking room.

Wieviel kostet das Zimmer pro Tag?
How much is the daily rate?

Akzeptieren Sie Kreditkarten?
Do you accept credit cards?

ACCOMMODATIONS

Welche Kreditkarten akzeptieren Sie?
Which credit cards do you accept?

Können Sie mein Gepäck aufs Zimmer bringen?
Can you bring my luggage to my room?

Wann gibt es Frühstück?
When is breakfast?

Bitte wecken Sie mich um _____ Uhr.
Please wake me up at _____ o'clock.

... funktioniert nicht.
... doesn't work.

>   **Das Licht ...**
>   The light ...

>   **Die Lampe ...**
>   The lamp ...

>   **Der Fernseher ...**
>   The television ...

>   **Die Klimaanlage ...**
>   The air-conditioning ...

>   **Der Aufzug ...**
>   The elevator ...

>   **Das Telefon ...**
>   The telephone ...

>   **Der Kühlschrank ...**
>   The refrigerator ...

Der Wasserhahn ...
The faucet ...

Die Toilette ...
The toilet ...

Ich habe / Wir haben keinen Strom.
I / We don't have electricity.

Kann ich / Können wir ...
Can I / Can we ...

... Frühstück auf dem Zimmer haben?
... have breakfast in the room?

... noch eine Bettdecke haben?
... have an extra blanket?

... noch ein Kissen haben?
... have another cushion?

... ein anderes Zimmer haben?
... have a different room?

Ich brauche / Wir brauchen ...
I / We need ...

... Toilettenpapier.
... toilet paper.

... Seife.
... soap.

... einen Föhn.
... a hair dryer.

ACCOMMODATIONS

... einen Aschenbecher.
... an ashtray.

... saubere Bettwäsche.
... clean sheets.

Es ist niemand an der Rezeption.
There's no one at the reception desk.

Mein / Unser Zimmer ist ...
My / Our room is ...

... nicht sauber.
... not clean.

... zu laut.
... too noisy.

Wann ist das Schwimmbad geöffnet?
When is the swimming pool open?

Ich habe meinen Zimmerschlüssel verloren.
I have lost my key.

Wo ist bitte die Dusche?
Where is the shower, please?

Wo ist bitte die Toilette?
Where is the toilet, please?

Ich möchte etwas in die Reinigung geben!
I have some laundry to do!

Können Sie mir das bitte bügeln?
Could you please iron this?

Ich möchte / Wir möchten bitte bezahlen!
I / We would like to pay, please!

Hier muß ein Fehler vorliegen!
This must be a mistake!

Das kann nicht sein!
That's not possible!

Können Sie mir bitte ein Taxi bestellen?
Could you call a taxi for me?

➤ Food and Drink

German cuisine is said to be very greasy and heavy and some people say that most dishes only consist of meat and potatoes. That statement, of course, is as true as the European prejudice that Americans only eat hamburgers. Dishes vary in combinations, condiments and flavor from the north of Germany, where fish is an important part of everyday food, the central part of Germany with its innumerable varieties of sausages, southern Germany with its world famous Bavarian specialities (roast pork with potato dumplings), Austria where sweet dishes and cakes are famous (think of the *Sacher* in Vienna), to the diversity of Swiss cheeses and the cuisine of the Swiss Alps: heavy food for strong winters.

Many Oktoberfest-type events all over Germany, Austria, and Switzerland give one an opportunity to try the specialities—even the oddest ones, like tripe—and to experience the way people have fun: most start singing and end up drunk, just as in most parts of the world.

Germany is not only the home of world famous beers, but also of wines. The white wines, especially Riesling, from the Mosel region are some of the finest in the world.

Some of the most common dishes of German, Austrian and Swiss cuisines:

Braten
Bigger portions of meat roasted in the oven for several hours. Besides the below mentioned *Schweine-*

braten, there are *Kalbsbraten* (roast veal), *Gänsebraten* (roast goose), *Lambraten* (roast lamb), and *Enten- braten* (roast duck).

Schweinebraten
Roast pork, perhaps the most famous dish of German cuisine. Typical for Bavaria.

Brathähnchen
Roast chicken

Gaisburger Marsch
Bouillon-type soup with meat and vegetables. Typical for the southern part of Germany, especially Baden- Württemberg.

Strammer Max
Dish made of ground meat, fried egg, and fried pota- toes. Typical for northern Germany.

Flammkuchen
Southern German type of pizza, but with *speck* (bacon) and sour cream instead of tomatoes and cheese. It is originally a speciality of the Alsace region in the neighboring part of France.

Gulasch
Goulash. Though originally Hungarian, this dish has been assimilated by Germans and Austrians as a national dish.

Wiener Schnitzel
A thin slice of veal, fried in breadcrumbs. This is one of the most popular meat dishes. It is usually served with French fries or potato salad.

FOOD AND DRINK

Wiener / Frankfurter Würstel (or Würstchen); Saitenwürste

Slim sausage that is not fried but boiled. It is popular everywhere in Germany, Austria and Switzerland. The interesting thing is that in Vienna it is called *Frankfurter Würstel*, but in Frankfurt *Wiener Würstel*. *Saitenwürstel* is just another name for it.

Lyoner

Wiener Würstel-type sausage, but much thicker.

Kutteln

Tripe. In southern Germany prepared in a vinegar sauce ... for whomever likes it ...

Knödel / Klöße

Dumplings made from either raw and/or cooked potatoes or from bread.

Salads appear in many varieties: from noodle salad and rice salad to tomato or lettuce salads. Typical varieties are:

Kartoffelsalat

Potato salad, popular with above mentioned *Würstel*.

Fleischsalat

Meat salad, made of Lyoner sausage, sour cream, mayonnaise, and cucumber. *Ochsenmaulsalat* is a special kind of *Fleischsalat*, but instead of Lyoner sausage the meat of the mouth of oxen is used.

Käsefondue

Fondue made from several types of Swiss cheese, white wine, and garlic. A famous Swiss dish.

Pommes Frites
The French expression is used for french fries.

Rösti
Swiss dish prepared from grated potatoes (hash browns).

Bratkartoffeln
Fried potatoes are very popular as a side dish.

Palatschinken
Like the Gulasch, this Austrian speciality is of Hungarian origin. *Palatschinken* are very thin pancakes. They come rolled up with a variety of fillings.

Kaiserschmarrn
An Austrian sweet dish, prepared from eggs, raisins, and flour. One of the famous Austrian desserts.

Apfelstrudel
Another one of the famous Austrian sweet dishes. This one is prepared with rum-soaked grated apples, raisins, and almonds, rolled and baked in paper-thin pastry.

In the Restaurant

In Europe you do not usually wait to be seated, just look around for a table that you would like, or ask the waiter. After you have asked for the menu the waiter will leave you alone for a while and then come back to take your orders.

Wohin kann ich mich setzen? / Wohin könne wir uns setzen?
Where can I / we take a seat?

FOOD AND DRINK

Einen Tisch für Raucher / Nichtraucher, bitte!
A smokers / non-smokers table, please!

Kann ich bitte die Speisekarte sehen?
Could I see the menu please?
Was hätten Sie gerne?
What would you like to have?

Wieviel kostet das?
How much is that?

Ich würde / Wie würden gerne bestellen!
I'd like / We'd like to give our orders!

Ich hätte gerne ...
I will have ...

Kann ich _____ (1) anstelle _____ (2) haben?
Could I have _____ (1) instead of _____ (2)?

Das Essen schmeckt mir nicht.
I don't like my food.

Es ist ...
It is ...

> **... kalt.**
> ... cold.

> **... zu salzig.**
> ... too salty.

> **... zu scharf.**
> ... too hot.

> **... schlecht.**
> ... bad.

... lecker.
... delicious.

Ich brauche ... / Wir brauchen ...
I would like to have ... / We need ...

... (noch) eine Serviette.
... (another) napkin.

... (noch) eine Gabel.
... (another) fork.

... (noch) ein Messer.
... (another) knife.

... (noch) einen Löffel.
... (another) spoon.

... (noch) einen Teller.
... (another) plate.

... (noch) ein Glas.
... (another) glass.

... (noch) eine Tasse.
... (another) cup.

Ich hätte gerne ...
I'd like to have ...

... einen Kaffee.
... a coffee.

... einen Nachtisch.
... a dessert.

... ein Glas / eine Flasche Wein.
... a glass / a bottle of wine.

... ein Glas / eine Flasche Bier.
... a glass / a bottle of beer.

... ein Glass / eine Flasche Mineralwasser.
... a glass / a bottle of mineral water.

Toilets are usually marked by pictograms or by the word *Herren* for the gentlemen's room, or *Damen* for the ladies' room.

Wo ist die Toilette bitte?
Where's the restroom, please?

People usually leave some tip (ca. 10% of the bill), but it is not obligatory.

Die Rechnung, bitte!
The bill, please!

Getrennte Rechnungen, bitte!
Separate bills, please!

Alles zusammen.
All together on one bill.

➤ Communications

Most hotels have a telephone in every room and fax service at the reception desk, and will handle your mail. Computer terminals for e-mail access are not usually found in hotels, but are available in luxury class hotels.

Ich möchte Briefmarken kaufen.
I want to buy stamps.

Wieviel kostet ein Brief innerhalb Deutschlands / innerhalb Europas / in die USA?
How much is a letter within Germany / within Europe / to the United States?

Ich muß das nach ... schicken.
I need to send this to ...

Die Briefmarke - stamp

Der Brief - letter

Die Postkarte - postcard

Das Paket - parcel

Luftpost - airmail

Normale Post - surface mail

Das Porto - postage

Wo kann ich telefonieren?
Where can I make a telephone call?

COMMUNICATIONS

Wieviel kostet eine Minute nach Amerika?
How much does one minute cost to the United States?

Wo kann ich meine e-mails abrufen?
Where can I get my e-mail?

Von wo kann ich ein Fax schicken?
Where can I send a fax?

Haben Sie einen Internetanschluß?
Do you have Internet access?

Kann ich hier meine e-mails abrufen?
Can I check my e-mail here?

➤ Money

The German currency is the Deutsche Mark (DM), that is divided into 100 Pfennig (Pf). Note that you don't say *Deutsche Mark* to name the currency, but *D Mark*, pronounced like "day mark."

The Austrian currency is the Schilling (ATS). A division into 100 Groschen exists, but it is not used today.

The Swiss currency is the Schweizer Franken (SFr), divided into 100 Rappen (Rp).

On January 1st 2002, Germany and Austria will join the monetary union of the European community. From this date on, the Deutsche Mark and Schilling will no longer exist. The official currency of all countries of the European community (excluding Great Britain) will then be the Euro (€), subdivided into 100 cents. Switzerland is not part of the European community and will keep its national currency.

Credit cards are widely accepted, but American, or U.S. checks can be used only in bank transactions. Most banks have electronic cashiers (ATMs), where you can get money from your credit card account. Citibank has many offices in Germany.

Wo kann ich Geld wechseln?
Where can I change money?

Ich möchte (etwas) Geld wechseln.
I'd like to change (some) money.

Können Sie mir diesen Schein in Kleingeld wechseln?

Could you change this bill into small money?

Kann ich Geld auf meine Kreditkarte bekommen?

Can I get money on my credit card?

Wie ist der Kurs? / Wechselkurs?

How is the rate? / exchange rate?

Ich möchte _____ Dollar in D-Mark / Schilling / Franken / Euro wechseln.

I want to change US$ _____ into German marks / Swiss franks / Austrian shillings / euro.

Berechnen Sie eine Kommission?

Is there a commission fee?

Bitte geben Sie mir eine Quittung.

Please give me a receipt.

Sind Sie sicher, daß das stimmt?

Are you sure that's right?

Bitte geben Sie mir auch etwas Kleingeld.

Please also give me some change.

➤ Doing Business

Ich möchte eine _____ abhalten.
I would like to have a _____.

   ... Konferenz.
   ... conference.

   ... Sitzung / Besprechung.
   ... meeting.

Habe Sie einen Sitzungsraum?
Do you have a conference room?

   ... für _____ Personen.
   ... for _____ persons.

Konferenztisch - conference table

Computer - computer

Stuhl - chair

Drucker - printer

Schreibmaschine - typewriter

Wir benötigen ...
We need ...

   ... ein Büro.
   ... an office.

   ... einen Projektor.
   ... a projector.

DOING BUSINESS

... Getränke.
... drinks.

... ein Mikrofon.
... a microphone.

... Papier.
... paper.

... Stifte.
... pens.

... Bleistifte.
... pencils.

... Radiergummis.
... erasers.

➤ Economy

In Europe, the economy is organized similarly to the United States economy, but company structures are very different.

Popular forms of commercial entities are:

GmbH - **Gesellschaft mit beschränkter Haftung** = Limited Liability Company

KG - **Kommanditgesellschaft** = Limited Commercial Partnership

AG - **Aktiengesellschaft** = stock corporation

Another popular form is the GmbH & Co. KG, which is a limited commercial partnership (KG) formed with a limited liability company (GmbH) as general partner and the members of the GmbH, their families or investors, as limited partners. There is no U.S. equivalent to such a construction.

Wirtschaft - economy

Aktienkurs - share rate

Zinssatz - interest rate

Beteiligung - investment, holding

Geschäftsbericht - management report

Finanzierung - financing, funding

Fonds, Investmentfonds - fund

Kredit - credit, loan

Filialen - branches

Branche - industrial sector

➤ Shopping

Shops are open from 9:00 or 10:00 A.M. to 6:00 or 8:00 P.M. in Germany, Austria and Switzerland. Shops are closed on Sundays in all three countries. In many places in Switzerland shops are closed on Monday mornings, and open only at 3:00 P.M. Shopping centers are usually found downtown. In most shops you can exchange bought items during the days after the acquisition, but it is better to ask to be sure. Credit cards are widely accepted.

Ich möchte ... kaufen.
I want to buy ... .

Ich schaue mich nur um!
I'm just looking!

Wo kann ich ... kaufen?
Where can I buy ... ?

Können Sie mir ... zeigen?
Can you show me ... ?

Wieviel kostet das?
How much is it?

Ich nehme das!
I'll take that!

Clothing

Ich möchte das anprobieren.
I would like to try that on.

Es ist mir zu ... .
It's too ... for me.

> **... groß**
> ... big

> **... klein**
> ... small

> **... eng**
> ... tight

> **... weit**
> ... loose

> **... lang**
> ... long

> **... kurz**
> ... short

Es paßt mir.
It fits well.

Habe Sie das eine Nummer kleiner / größer?
Do you have this in one size smaller / bigger?

Haben Sie das in einer anderen Größe?
Do you have that in another size?

Haben Sie das mit einem anderen Muster?
Do you have that in another style?

Haben Sie das in einer anderen Farbe?
Do you have this in another color?

Kann ich das zurückgeben?
Can I return this?

Pullover - sweater

Hemd - shirt

T-Shirt - t-shirt

Hose - pants

Jeans - jeans

Unterwäsche - underwear

Unterhose - slip

Unterhemd - undershirt

Socken - socks

Strümpfe - stockings

Schuhe - shoes

Badehose - bathing trunks

Regenmantel - raincoat

Schreibwaren - stationary

Buch - book

Wörterbuch - dictionary

Englische Bücher - English books

Stifte - pens

Kugelschreiber - ballpoint pen

Bleistift - pencil

Papier - paper

Briefumschläge - envelopes

Postkarten - postcards

Batterie / Batterien - battery / batteries

Briefmarken - stamps

At the Photo Shop

Ich möchte bitte einen Film.
I want film / a roll of film, please.

Bitte entwickeln Sie mir diesen Film!
Please develop this roll of film!

Wann werden die Bilder fertig sein?
When will the pictures be ready?

Souvenirs

Popular souvenirs from Germany, Austria, or Switzerland include cuckoo clocks, leather pants, beer glasses, cheese, and other Alps-related items. But other regions have their own traditions, and by looking out carefully you will be able to find many beautiful local products.

Können Sie mir das nach Hause schicken?
Can you send this directly to my home?

Souvenirgeschäft - souvenir shop

Kiosk - newsstand

Schreibwarengeschäft - stationer's

Uhrmacher - watchmaker

Juwelier - jewelry store

Kuckucksuhr - cuckoo clock

Bierkrug - beer glass

Bayrische Lederhosen - Bavarian leatherpants

Schmuck - jewelry

Armband - bracelet

Ring - ring

Kette / Halskette - necklace

Ohrringe - earrings

➤ Sightseeing and Entertainment

Most European cities have over 400 years of history and some have over 1500. During World War II the historical centers of many major cities were destroyed, but most have been successively reconstructed over the following decades. Small medieval cities of exquisite beauty are preserved in a remarkable state, like **Rothenburg ob der Tauber** and **Heidelberg** in Germany, **Bern** in Switzerland, and **Salzburg** in Austria.

Since the reunification of West and East Germany, the cities of Eastern Germany have also been reconstructed. East German cities like **Leipzig** and **Dresden** are now major tourist attractions. In Austria, cities like **Melk** or **Linz** are focuses of the famous Austrian baroque architecture. Other cities—**Vienna (Wien)**, **Salzburg**, **Munich (München)**, **Hamburg, Berlin**—stand for themselves.

Every major city in Germany, Austria, and Switzerland has interesting museums of art and culture, history, technical development, and many other themes. Some of the most famous, interesting, and beautiful museums are:

München (Munich):
Alte Pinakothek (arts)
Neue Pinakothek (arts)
Deutsches Museum (technical history and development, one of the greatest museums in Germany)

Stuttgart:
Staatsgalerie (arts)

Wien (Vienna):
Kunsthistorisches Museum (arts)
Naturhistorisches Museum (natural history)

Hamburg:
Kunsthalle (arts)

Berlin:
Pergamonmuseum (Ancient Egyptian art)
Naturkundemuseum (Natural history)

Köln:
Römisch-Germanisches Museum (Roman-Germanic history)

Düsseldorf:
Kunstsammlung Nordrhein-Westfalen (arts)

Stralsund:
Schiffahrtsmuseum (Naval museum)

Dresden:
Grünes Gewölbe (jewelry and art collection of the Saxon emperors)

Note that most museums are closed on Mondays.

Wo ist bitte das _____ - Museum?
Where is the _____ - museum, please?

Gibt es hier ein ...
Does this city have a ...

   ... technisches Museum?
   ... technical museum?

... Kunstmuseum?
... art gallery?

... ethnographisches Museum?
... ethnological museum?

... interessantes Museum?
... interesting museum?

Ist das Museum heute geöffnet?
Is the museum open today?

Wann öffnet das Museum?
When does the museum open?

Wieviel kostet der Eintritt?
How much is the entrance fee?

Gibt es einen Museumskatalog?
Do you have a catalog of the museum?

Ich möchte einen Museumskatalog, bitte!
I want a catalog of the museum, please!

Gibt es besondere Sehenswürdigkeiten in dieser Stadt?
Are there special tourist attractions in this city?

Wo ist bitte ...
Where is ...

... die Touristeninformation?
... the tourist information office?

... das Stadtzentrum?
... the city center?

... das Opernhaus?
... the opera house?

... das Theater?
... the theater?

... das Stadion?
... the stadium?

... das Schloß?
... the castle?

... die _____ - Kirche / der Dom?
... the _____ - church / the dome?

Most cities not only have movie theaters, but also an opera house and dramatic theaters.

Was gibt es heute in der Oper / im Theater / im Kino?
What's on tonight at the opera / the theater / the movies?

Wo kann ich Eintrittskarten für _____ kaufen?
Where can I buy tickets for _____?

Was kostet eine Eintrittskarte für _____?
How much is a ticket for _____?

Ich möchte eine Eintrittskarte für _____.
I want a ticket for _____.

Ich möchte zwei / drei Eintrittskarten für _____.
I want two / three tickets for _____.

Gibt es eine Nachmittagsvorstellung?
Is there an afternoon show?

Um wieviel Uhr beginnt die Vorstellung?
When does the show begin?

Ich möchte einen guten Patz!
I want a good seat!

Gibt es Filme in englischer Sprache?
Are there movies in the English language?

Wo gibt es eine ...
Where is a ...

> **... Cocktailbar?**
> ... cocktail bar?

> **... Diskothek?**
> ... club?

> **... gutes Restaurant?**
> ... good restaurant?

> **... Kneipe?**
> ... pub?

> **... Einkaufszentrum?**
> ... shopping center?

> **... ein Schwimmbad?**
> ... a public pool?

➤ Nature

The landscapes of Germany, Austria and Switzerland vary from flatlands to the high mountains of the Alps. Tourists can find virtually every type of environment—except for tropical forests.

Trekking is popular not only in the German, Austrian, and Swiss Alps, but also in the other mountainous regions of southern and middle Germany, like the **Schwäbische Alb**, situated between Stuttgart and Ulm and southern Germany, or the **Sächsische Schweiz**, near Dresden (Saxonia) in middle Germany.

Das Gebirge - the mountains

Die Alpen - the Alps

Berge - mountains

Hügel - hills

See - lake

Meer - ocean

Wald - forest

Sumpf - swamp

Wiese - meadow

Fluß - river

Bauernhof - farm

Feld - field

Vieh - cattle

Ich würde gerne einen Ausflug machen.
I would like to go on a trip.

Ich möchte eine Wanderung unternehmen.
I would like to go hiking.

Kann man hier in der Gegend wandern gehen?
Is it possible to go hiking here? (see section "Recreation")

Können Sie mir / uns einen schönen Wanderweg empfehlen?
Can you recommend me / us an interesting hike?

Ist es gefährlich?
Is it dangerous?

➤ Recreation, Sports, and Hobbies

You will find ways to relax and opportunities to play different sports everywhere. Europeans have different preferences in sports. American football, for example, is not widespread, while soccer is very popular.

Many hotels, especially those of the four and five-star category, have gyms and tennis courts. Every city has public pools where you can go swimming.

Schwimmbad - public pool

Schwimmbecken - swimming pool

Tennisplatz - tennis court

Fitneßstudio - gym

Squash - squash

Golf - golf

Jogging - jogging

Leichtathletik - track and field

Massage - massage

Fußball - soccer

Tischtennis - table tennis

American Football - American football

Billard - pool

Kann ich einen ... ausleihen?
Can I borrow a ...?

> **... Tennisschläger**
> ... tennis racket

> **... Tischtennisschläger**
> ... table tennis racket

> **... Badeanzug**
> ... swimsuit

> **... Golfschläger**
> ... golf club

Gibt es hier einen Golfplatz?
Is there a golf course somewhere here?

Kann ich eine ...- Ausrüstung mieten?
Can I rent a ...- equipment?

Ich möchte einen schönen Spaziergang machen!
I would like to go for a nice walk!

Wo kann ich einen Spaziergang machen?
Where can I go for a walk?

Ich möchte eine Wanderung unternehmen.
I would like to go hiking.

Ich brauche feste Schuhe.
I need tight shoes.

Ist es gefährlich?
Is it dangerous?

➤ Religion and Spirit

Ich möchte einen Gottesdienst / eine Synagoge besuchen.
I would like to go to church / to a synagogue.

Ich suche eine ...
I am looking for a ...

> **... Kirche.**
> ... church.

> **... Moschee.**
> ... mosque.

> **... Synagoge.**
> ... synagogue.

Um wieviel Uhr beginnt der nächste Gottesdienst?
At what time does the next service begin?

Um wieviel Uhr beginnt die nächste Messe?
At what time does the next mass begin?

Um wieviel Uhr sind morgen die Gottesdienste?
When are the services tomorrow morning?

Ich bin ...
I am ...

> **... evangelisch.**
> ... protestant.

> **... katholisch.**
> ... catholic.

... orthodox.
... orthodox.

... anglikanisch.
... anglican.

... presbyterianisch.
... presbyterian.

... Muslim.
... Muslim.

... Buddhist.
... Buddhist.

... nicht religiös.
... not religious.

➤ Government

All European states are governed democratically. Germany, Austria, and Switzerland are federal republics with governments on the state and federal levels, but the governmental structure is quite different from the American one. States are called *Bundesländer* in Germany and Austria, and *Kantone* in Switzerland. The position that is equivalent to United States governor is called *Ministerpräsident* in Germany, and *Landeshauptmann* in Austria, but they have less power. The same is true for the equivalent of the United States president's position, which is called *Bundeskanzler* in Germany and *Bundespräsident* in Austria and Switzerland. The Swiss *Bundespräsident*, however, has no more power than any member of the congress, the *Bundesrat*. The president of Germany has not much more than representational power.

Politicians who are members of the Bundestag or the state parliaments are elected for the *Bundestag* (D), the *Nationalrat* (A), or the *Bundesrat* (CH) (congress) for a period of 4 years. In Germany the Bundestag elects the *Bundeskanzler*. The Austrian *Bundespräsident* is elected for a period of six years, and the Swiss *Bundespräsident* only for one year.

Bundestag (D) / Nationalrate (A) / Bundesversammlung (CH) - congress

Bundeskanzler - chancellor

Bundespräsident - president

Ministerium - ministry

Minister - minister

GOVERNMENT

Außenministerium - State Department

Außenminister - Secretary of State

Innenministerium - Department of the Interior

Innenminister - Secretary of the Interior

Finanzministerium - Treasury Department

Finanzminister - Secretary of Treasury

Justizministerium - Department of Justice

Justizminister - Attorney General

Verkehrsministerium - Department of Transportation

Amt - agency, bureau, office

Amt für öffentliche Ordnung - Bureau of public services

Einwohnermeldeamt - residents' registration office

Verfassung - constitution

Kommunismus - communism

Demokratie - democracy

Menschenrechte - human rights

Wahlen - elections

Opposition - opposition

Politiker – politician

➤ **Health and Hygiene**

Drugstores are called *Drogerie* and pharmacies *Apotheke,* but unlike in the United States, drugstores do not sell medications, only general household and beauty products. Pharmacies usually have a counter where you are assisted by a pharmacist. You can buy light medications (such as aspirin or cough relief) without a prescription (*Rezept*), but heavier medications (such as antibiotics or cortisone) are only sold with a doctor's prescription.

Hygienic conditions are generally very good in central Europe. You can find clean toilets everywhere, with the exception of ones at motorway gas stations, which should be avoided if possible.

Gibt es hier eine Toilette?
Is there a toilet somewhere here?

Wo ist die Toilette, bitte?
Where's the toilet, please?

Ich brauche Toilettenpapier.
I need toilet paper.

Gibt es hier eine Dusche?
Is there a shower somewhere here?

Die Toilette / Dusche ist schmutzig.
The toilet / shower is dirty.

Ich brauche ...
I need ...

Ich möchte ...
I want ...

... Verhütungsmittel.
... contraceptives.

... Kondome.
... condoms.

... Vitamintabletten.
... vitamins.

... Tampons.
... tampons.

... Damenbinden.
... sanitary napkins.

... Seife.
... soap.

... Zahnpasta.
... toothpaste.

... eine Zahnbürste.
... a toothbrush.

... Rasierklingen.
... razor blades.

... Shampoo.
... shampoo.

... Parfüm.
... perfume.

... Lippenstift.
... lipstick.

... Makeup.
... makeup.

... Sonnencreme.
... suntan lotion.

... Haarspray.
... hairspray.

Since shops are open only from 9:00 or 10:00 A.M. to 6:00 or 8:00 P.M., pharmacies are not usually open at night, but in every city at least one pharmacy stays open. This service is called *Nachtapotheke*. On every pharmacy's door there is a sign that tells you which pharmacy is open at night on a specific weekday, including address and telephone number. Furthermore, every hospital has night services. Most doctors and other people working in the health sector speak English.

Ich brauche einen Arzt / Zahnarzt.
I need to see a doctor / dentist.

Ich brauche einen Arzt, der Englisch spricht!
I need a doctor who speaks English!

Mein Freund / Meine Freundin ist krank!
My friend *(m/f)* is sick!

Ich brauche einen Krankenwagen.
I need an ambulance.

Kann der Doktor in mein Hotel kommen?
Can the doctor come to my hotel?

HEALTH AND HYGIENE

Ich muß ins Krankenhaus!
I need to go to the hospital!

The following sentences indicate the part of your body that hurts:

... tut weh.
… hurts.

> **Mein Herz ...**
> My heart …
>
> **Mein Magen ...**
> My stomach …
>
> **Meine Leber ...**
> My liver …
>
> **Mein Arm ...**
> My arm …
>
> **Meine Brust ...**
> My chest …
>
> **Mein (rechtes / linkes) Auge ...**
> My (right / left) eye …
>
> **Mein Kopf ...**
> My head …
>
> **Meine Ohren ...**
> My ears …
>
> **Mein Bein ...**
> My leg …

Mein Fuß ...
My foot ...

Meine Hand ...
My hand ...

Das Jelenk ...
The joint ...

Mein Handgelenk ...
My wrist ...

Meine Schulter ...
My shoulder ...

Mein Hals ...
My neck ...

Ich bin allergisch gegen ...
I'm allergic to ...

Er / Sie ist allergisch gegen ...
He / She is allergic to ...

Ich bin schwanger!
I'm pregnant!

Sie ist schwanger!
She's pregnant!

You can use the following sentences either to indicate
the part that is hurting, or to ask for a medication or
remedy for it:

Ich habe ...
I have ...

Ich möchte etwas gegen ...
I want something for ...

... Kopfschmerzen.
... a headache.

... Magenschmerzen.
... a stomachache.

... einen Kater.
... a hangover.

... Zahnschmerzen.
... a toothache.

... Asthma.
... asthma.

... hohen / niedrigen Blutdruck.
... high / low blood pressure.

... Diabetes.
... diabetes.

... einen Sonnenbrand.
... a sunburn.

... Grippe.
... a flu.

... eine Erkältung.
... a cold.

... Halsschmerzen.
... a sore throat.

... Durchfall.
... diarrhea.

... Fieber.
... fever.

... Ohrenschmerzen.
... earache.

... eine Vergiftung.
... a poisoning.

... eine Verstopfung.
... indigestion.

... Übelkeit.
... nausea.

Ich möchte ...
I want ...

... Tabletten.
... tablets / pills.

... Tropfen.
... drops.

... eine Spritze.
... a shot.

... Zäpfchen.
... a suppository.

... eine Salbe.
... a cream.

HEALTH AND HYGIENE

Mir ist schlecht.
I have nausea.

Ich muß mich übergeben.
I have to throw up.

Ich fühle mich, als ob ich mich immer übergeben müßte.
I feel like vomiting all the time.

Ich möchte ...
I want ...

   ... ein Antibiotikum / Antihistamin.
   ... an antibiotic / antihistamine.

   ... Beruhigungsmittel.
   ... a tranquilizer.

In the dentist's office you might need the following sentences:

Ich möchte eine Spritze.
I want a shot.

Ich möchte eine provisorische Füllung.
I want a temporary filling.

For beauty care you might need the following phrases:

Wo kann ich zum Friseur gehen?
Where can I have my hair done?

Bitte waschen und schneiden!
Please shampoo and cut!

Bitte waschen und legen!
Please shampoo and set!

Ich möchte ...
I want ...

... eine Massage.
... a massage.

... eine Maniküre.
... a manicure.

... eine Pediküre.
... a pedicure.

... Locken.
... curls.

... eine Dauerwelle.
... a permanent.

➤ Emergency

In case of an emergency you can always call the emergency hotline number **110** for free from any telephone, including cellular phones.

Ich brauche Hilfe!
I need help!

Können Sie uns / mir bitte helfen?
Can you help me / us please?

Darf ich bitte Ihr Telefon benutzen?
Could I use your telephone, please?

Rufen Sie schnell Hilfe!
Call help quickly!

Rufen Sie schnell ...
Call quickly ...

> **... einen Arzt!**
> ... a doctor!

> **... einen Krankenwagen!**
> ... an ambulance!

> **... die Polizei!**
> ... the police!

> **... die Feuerwehr!**
> ... the fire department!

Ich hatte / Wir hatten einen Unfall!
I had / We had an accident!

Ich bin verletzt!
I am injured!

Mein Freund / Meine Freundin ist verletzt!
My friend (m/f) is injured!

Es gibt Verletzte!
Some people were injured!

Ich brauche / Wir brauchen einen Arzt.
I need / We need to see a doctor.

Ich brauche einen Arzt, der Englisch spricht!
I need a doctor who speaks English.

Ich brauche / Wir brauchen einen Krankenwagen.
I need / We need an ambulance.

Ich brauche einen Dolmetscher!
I need a interpreter!

Ich bin allergisch gegen ...
I'm allergic to ...

Ich bin angegriffen worden!
I've been attacked!

Ich bin vergewaltigt worden!
I've been raped!

... ist gestohlen worden!
... has been stolen!

> **Mein Geldbeutel ...**
> My purse ...

Meine Papiere ...
My papers ...

Mein Geld ...
My money ...

Meine Handtasche ...
My handbag ...

Meine Kamera ...
My camera ...

Meine Fotoausrüstung ...
My camera equipment ...

Wo ist die amerikanische Botschaft?
Where's the U.S. embassy?

Wo ist das amerikanische Konsulat?
Where's the U.S. consulate?

Ich möchte den amerikanischen Botschafter / Konsul sprechen!
I want to speak to the U.S. ambassador / consul!

➤ Numbers

German numbers are simple to form. The numbers 10 to 20 are combinations of the numbers 1 to 10 and the word *zehn* (ten). Exceptions are the numbers 11 and 12. From twenty on, the structure of German numerals is always like "one-and-twenty," for 21, or "six-and-forty," for 46.

Ordinal numbers (ex. first, second, eighth, etc.) are formed by adding *te* or *ste* to the word: fifth is *fünfte*, fourteenth is *vierzehnte*, twentieth is *zwanzigste*. The ending *ste* is generally used where it sounds better acoustically. Ordinal numbers remain the same in all genders. They are capitalized when used as nouns.

1	6
eins	sechs
first	sixth
erste	sechste
2	7
zwei	sieben
second	seventh
zweite	siebte
3	8
drei	acht
third	eighth
dritte	achte
4	9
vier	neun
fourth	ninth
vierte	neunte
5	10
fünf	zehn
fifth	tenth
fünfte	zehnte

11	21
elf	einundzwanzig
eleventh	twenty-first
elfte	einundzwanzigste
12	22
zwölf	zweiundzwanzig
twelfth	twenty-second
zwölfte	zweiundzwanzigste
13	30
dreizehn	dreißig
thirteenth	thirtieth
dreizehnte	dreißigste
14	40
vierzehn	vierzig
fourteenth	fortieth
vierzehnte	vierzigste
15	46
fünfzehn	sechsundvierzig
fifteenth	forty-sixth
fünfzehnte	sechsundvierzigste
16	50
sechzehn	fünfzig
sixteenth	fiftieth
sechzehnte	fünfzigste
17	60
siebzehn	sechzig
seventeenth	sixtieth
siebzehnte	sechzigste
18	70
achtzehn	siebzig
eighteenth	seventieth
achtzehnte	siebzigste
19	80
neunzehn	achtzig
nineteenth	eightieth
neunzehnte	achtzigste
20	90
zwanzig	neunzig
twentieth	ninetieth
zwanzigste	neunzigste

100
hundert
one hundredth
hundertste
110
hundertzehn
one hundred and tenth
hundertzehnte
120
hundertzwanzig
one hundred and twentieth
hundertzwanzigste
123
hundertdreiundzwanzig
one hundred and twenty-third
hundertdreiundzwanzigste
200
zweihundert
two hundredth
zweihundertste
1,000
tausend
one thousandth
tausendste
10,000
zehntausend
ten thousandth
zehntausendste
100,000
hunderttausend
one hundred thousandth
hunderttausendste
1,000,000
eine Million
one millionth
millionste

Age

Wie alt sind Sie / Wie alt bist Du?
How old are you? (polite / familiar)

Ich bin ...
I am ...

> **... _____ Jahre alt.**
> ... _____ years old.

> **... volljährig.**
> ... an adult.

> **... jünger als ...**
> ... younger than ...

> **... alter als ...**
> ... older than ...

Sind Sie volljährig? / Bist Du volljährig?
Are you an adult? (polite / familiar)

➤ Measurements

In Europe, inches, pounds, and miles are only used in Great Britain. The rest of Europe follows the metric system, using measurements of meters and grams.

You can find conversion tables in the back of this book.

Abbreviations

Distances:

mm - **Millimeter**: millimeter (1/1000 meter)
cm - **Zentimeter**: centimeter (1/100 meter)
m - **Meter**: meter
km - **Kilometer**: kilometer (1000 meters)

Weights:

g - **Gramm**: gram
kg - **Kilogramm** or **Kilo**: kilogram (1000 grams)
t - **Tonne**: ton (1000 kg)
0.5 kg (= 1 **Pfund**) (The metric pound is rarely used.)

Speed:

km/h - **Kilometer pro Stunde**: kilometers per hour

Conversion:

1 cm = 0.39 inches
1 inch = 2.54 cm

MEASUREMENTS

1 m = 3.28 feet
1 ft = .03 meters

1 km = 1000 m = 0.62 miles
1 mile = 1.61 km

1 kg = 1000 g = 2.2 pounds
1 pound = 0.45 kg

1 l = 1.1 quart = 0.26 gallons = 2.11 pints
1 quart = 0.91 l
1 gallon = 3.85 l
1 pint = 0.47 l

➤ Time

In German, time is expressed "the other way around" than in English. Instead of saying "it is a quarter past three," Germans say "it is quarter four" (translated literally). This sounds strange but it is easy to understand: it is not yet four, only a certain degree, being 25 percent, i. e. a quarter. Just imagine that from the hour preceding the one talked about one quarter has already past. The same goes for "a quarter to four": Germans say "it is three quarters four."

Observe that in Europe the hours of the day are usually counted from 0:00 to 24:00, and not from 0:00 to 12:00 A.M. and P.M. Accordingly 4:00 P.M. in Europe is 16:00.

Wieviel Uhr ist es bitte?
What time is it please?

Wann können wir uns treffen?
When can we meet?

Es ist ...
It is ...

Wir können uns um ... treffen.
We can meet at ...

  ... 4 (Uhr).
  ... 4 (o'clock).

  ... halb 5 (Uhr).
  ... half past four (o'clock).

... viertel (1/4) nach 6 (Uhr) / viertel (1/4) 7 (Uhr).

... a quarter past 6 (o'clock).

... dreiviertel (3/4) 2 (Uhr) / viertel (1/4) vor 2 (Uhr).

... a quarter to 2 (o'clock).

... 17 (Uhr).

... 5 (o'clock) P.M.

Morgen - morning

Vormittag - morning (the time between early morning and noon)

Mittag - noon

Nachmittag - afternoon

Abend - evening

Nacht - night

Mitternacht - midnight

Gestern - yesterday

Vorgestern - the day before yesterday

Morgen - tomorrow

Übermorgen - the day after tomorrow

Später - later

Früher - sooner / earlier

Immer - always

Nie / Niemals - never

Manchmal - sometimes

Oft - often

Jahr - year

Monat - month

Tag - day

Stunde - hour

Minute - minute

Sekunde - second

Days of the Week

Montag - Monday

Dienstag - Tuesday

Mittwoch - Wednesday

Donnerstag - Thursday

Freitag - Friday

Samstag - Saturday

Sonntag - Sunday

Months of the Year

Januar - January

Februar - February

März - March

April - April

Mai - May

Juni - June

Juli - July

August - August

September - September

Oktober - October

November - November

Dezember - December

➤ Conversion Tables

Temperature

Celsius	Fahrenheit
–30°C	–22°F
–25°C	–13°F
–20°C	–4°F
–5°C	23°F
°C	32°F
5°C	41°F
10°C	50°F
15°C	59°F
20°C	68°F
25°C	77°F
30°C	86°F
35°C	95°F
40°C	104°F
45°C	113°F
50°C	122°F

CONVERSION TABLES

Distance

cm	inches
1	0,39
2	0,79
3	1,18
5	1,97
10	3,94
20	7,87
30	11,81
40	15,75
50	19,69
60	23,62
70	27,56
80	31,50
90	35,43
100	39,37

100 centimeters (cm) = 1 meter (m)

m	yards
1	1,09
2	2,19
3	3,28
5	5,47
10	10,94
20	21,87
30	32,81
40	43,74
50	54,68
100	109,36
200	218,72
300	328,08
500	546,80
800	874,88

1000 meters (m) = 1 kilometer (km)

CONVERSION TABLES

km	miles
1	0,62
5	3,11
10	6,21
20	12,43
50	31,07
100	62,14
200	124,28
500	310,69
1000	621,38

CONVERSION TABLES

Weight

grams	ounces
1	0,035
5	0,176
10	0,353
50	1,764
100	3,527
200	7,055
300	10,582
500	17,637
1000	35,273

1000 grams (g) = 1 kilograms (kg)

kilograms	pounds
1	0,56
2	1,13
5	2,82
10	5,64
20	11,29
30	16,93
40	22,57
50	28,22
60	33,86
70	39,51
80	45,15
90	50,79
100	56,44
200	112,87
300	169,31
500	282,19
1000	564,37

Volume

liters	pints	quarts	gallons
0,5	1,06	0,53	0,13
1	2,11	1,06	0,26
2	4,23	2,11	0,53
3	6,34	3,17	0,79
5	10,57	5,28	1,32
10	21,13	10,57	2,64
20	42,27	21,13	5,28
30	63,40	31,70	7,93
50	105,67	52,84	13,21
75	158,51	79,25	19,82
100	211,34	105,67	26,42
200	422,68	211,34	52,84
1000	2113,40	1056,70	264,20

Sometimes you see ml = milliliter = 1/1000 liter.

Dictionary and Phrasebooks

Albanian-English/English-Albanian
2,000 entries • 186 pages • 3¾ x 7
0-7818-0793-X • $11.95pb • (498)

**Arabic-English/English-Arabic
(Eastern Arabic)**
2,200 entries • 142 pages • 3¾ x 7
0-7818-0685-2 • $11.95pb • (774)

Australian-English/English-Australian
1,500 entries • 131 pages • 3¾ x 7
0-7818-0539-2 • $11.95pb • (626)

Azerbaijani-English/English-Azerbaijani
2,000 entries • 176 pages • 3¾ x 7
0-7818-0684-4 • $11.95pb • (753)

Basque-English/English-Basque
1,500 entries • 206 pages • 3¾ x 7
0-7818-0622-4 • $11.95pb • (751)

Bosnian-English/English-Bosnian
1,500 entries • 171 pages • 3¾ x 7
0-7818-0596-1 • $11.95pb • (691)

Breton-English/English-Breton
1,500 entries • 176 pages • 3¾ x 7
0-7818-0540-6 • $11.95pb • (627)

British-American/American-British English
1,400 entries • 154 pages • 3¾ x 7
0-7818-0450-7 • $11.95pb • (247)

Chechen-English/English-Chechen
1,400 entries • 176 pages • 3¾ x 7
0-7818-0446-9 • $11.95pb • (183)

Croatian-English/English-Croatian
2,000 entries • 272 pages • 3¾ x 7
0-7818-0810-3 • $11.95pb • (111)

Esperanto-English/English-Esperanto
2,500 entries • 223 pages • 3¾ x 7
0-7818-0736-0 • $13.95pb • (309)

French-English/English-French
5,500 entries • 175 pages • 3¾ x 7
0-7818-0856-1 • $11.95pb • (128)

Georgian-English/English-Georgian
1,300 entries • 150 pages • 3¾ x 7
0-7818-0542-2 • $11.95pb • (630)

Greek-English/English-Greek
1,500 entries • 263 pages • 3¾ x 7
0-7818-0635-6 • $14.95pb • (715)

Hebrew-English/English-Hebrew
Romanized
5,500 entries • 210 pages • 3¾ x 7
0-7818-0811-1 • $11.95pb • (126)

Igbo-English/English-Igbo
2,500 entries • 186 pages • 3¾ x 7
0-7818-0661-5 • $11.95pb • (750)

Ilocano-English/English-Ilocano
7,000 entries • 269 pages • 5½ x 8½
0-7818-0642-9 • $14.95pb • (718)

Irish-English/English-Irish
1,400 entries • 71 pages • 3¾ x 7
0-87052-110-1 • $7.95pb • (385)

Italian-English/English-Italian
2,100 entries • 213 pages • 3¾ x 7
0-7818-0812-X • $11.95pb • (137)

Japanese-English/English-Japanese
Romanized
2,300 entries • 220 pages • 3¾ x 7
0-7818-0814-6 • $12.95pb • (205)

Lao-English/English-Lao
Romanized
2,500 entries • 198 pages • 3¾ x 7
0-7818-0858-8 • $12.95pb • (179)

Lingala-English/English-Lingala
2,200 entries • 120 pages • 3¾ x 7
0-7818-0456-6 • $11.95pb • (296)

Malagasy-English/English-Malagasy
2,500 entries • 171 pages • 3¾ x 7
0-7818-0843-X • $11.95pb • (256)

Maltese-English/English-Maltese
1,500 entries • 175 pages • 3¾ x 7
0-7818-0565-1 • $11.95pb • (697)

Maya-English/English-Maya (Yucatec)
1,500 entries • 180 pages • 3¾ x 7
0-7818-0859-6 • $12.95pb • (244)

**Pilipino-English/English-Pilipino
(Tagalog)**
2,200 entries • 186 pages • 3¾ x 7
0-7818-0451-5 • $11.95pb • (295)

Polish-English/English-Polish
6,000 entries • 252 pages • 5½ x 8½
0-7818-0134-6 • $11.95pb • (192)

Romansch-English/English-Romansch
1,800 entries • 193 pages • 5½ x 7
0-7818-0778-6 • $12.95pb • (316)

Russian-English/English-Russian
Revised
3,000 entries • 228 pages • 5½ x 8½
0-7818-0190-7 • $11.95pb • (597)

Shona-English/English-Shona
1,400 entries • 160 pages • 3¾ x 7
0-7818-0813-8 • $11.95pb • (167)

Slovak-English/English-Slovak
1,300 entries • 180 pages • 3¾ x 7
0-7818-0663-1 • $13.95pb • (754)

Somali-English/English-Somali
1,400 entries • 176 pages • 3¾ x 7
0-7818-0621-6 • $13.95pb • (755)

**Spanish-English/English-Spanish
(Latin American)**
2,000 entries • 250 pages • 3¾ x 7
0-7818-0773-5 • $11.95pb • (261)

Tajik-English/English-Tajik
1,400 entries • 200 pages • 3¾ x 7
0-7818-0662-3 • $11.95pb • (752)

Thai-English/English-Thai
Romanized
1,800 entries • 197 pages • 3¾ x 7
0-7818-0774-3 • $12.95pb • (330)

Ukrainian-English/English-Ukrainian
3,000 entries • 205 pages • 5½ x 8½
0-7818-0188-5 • $11.95pb • (28)

Prices subject to change without prior notice. To order
Hippocrene Books, contact your local bookstore, call
(718) 454-2366, visit www.hippocrenebooks.com, or write
to: Hippocrene Books, 171 Madison Avenue, New York,
NY 10016. Please enclose check or money order adding
$5.00 shipping (UPS) for the first book and $.50 for each
additional title.